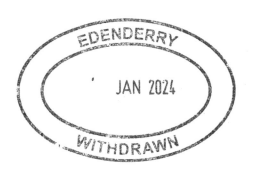

WOMEN WHO FLY

Other books by Lynn M. Homan and Thomas Reilly
Black Knights: The Story of the Tuskegee Airmen
The Tuskegee Airmen Story
Tuskegee Airmen: American Heroes
Girls Fly!

WOMEN WHO FLY

BY LYNN M. HOMAN
AND THOMAS REILLY

ILLUSTRATED BY
ROSALIE M. SHEPHERD

PELICAN PUBLISHING COMPANY
Gretna 2004

For Charlene, Lynn, and Abigail: the women who are important

—T. R.

For everyone, and especially Tom, who inspired me to write

—L. M. H.

The word "Pelican" and the depiction of a pelican are trademarks of Pelican Publishing Company, Inc., and are registered in the U.S. Patent and Trademark Office.

Library of Congress Cataloging-in-Publication Data

Homan, Lynn M.
  Women who fly / Lynn M. Homan and Thomas Reilly ; illustrated by Rosalie M. Shepherd.
    p. cm.
  Summary: Tells the stories of pioneering women who defied convention and made contributions to the field of aviation by becoming pilots and astronauts.
  ISBN 1-58980-160-1 (hardcover : alk. paper)
  1. Women air pilots—United States—Biography—Juvenile literature. 2. Air pilots—United States—Biography—Juvenile literature. [1. Air pilots. 2. Astronauts. 3. Women—Biography.] I. Reilly, Thomas. II. Shepherd, Rosalie M., ill. III. Title.

TL539.H614 2004
629.13'092'273—dc22

2003021538

Printed in the United States of America
Published by Pelican Publishing Company, Inc.
1000 Burmaster Street, Gretna, Louisiana 70053

Contents

Foreword

From the time I was a young girl, I loved to read books about flying and the pilots, who were so brave and adventurous. I read about Bobbi Trout, Ruth Law, Julia Clark, and the Stinson sisters. With fascination, I learned about the difficulties that American women faced during World War II when they sought to fly as members of the Women Airforce Service Pilots program. I rejoiced with their successes, as they proved that women have what it takes.

I admired the courage of women fliers such as Bessie Coleman and Amelia Earhart. The achievements of Jacqueline Cochran, Nancy Harkness Love, and Jerrie Cobb inspired me. I dreamed that one day I would follow in their footsteps. So many of their stories had almost been lost to history but have now been chronicled by Lynn Homan and Tom Reilly in *Women Who Fly*.

I can imagine the sense of elation that Harriet Quimby and Matilde Moisant, the first American women to receive their licenses to fly, must have felt. I know that elation firsthand. While attending the United States Air Force Test Pilot School, I was selected for NASA's astronaut program. In 1995, on STS-63 *Discovery*, I had the opportunity to be the first woman Space Shuttle pilot. Prior to the launch, several members of the Mercury 13 project came to Kennedy Space Center to offer encouragement and wish me luck. They were such an inspiration!

Then, just a few years later, as part of the STS-93 *Columbia* mission, I became the first woman to serve as Shuttle commander.

Undoubtedly, the successes of these history-making aviators have made it easier for women to pursue a career in aviation today. They have paved the way with their talent and determination.

Dreams and hopes are very important in life. Women such as Amelia Earhart, Bessie Coleman, and Jacqueline Cochran shared a common dream—they all desperately, often against tremendous obstacles, wanted to fly.

I've shared that dream. When I was a child, I dreamed about space. I admired pilots, astronauts, and explorers of all kinds. I wanted to someday be one of them. I hope that you will be inspired to reach for your dreams also, for dreams do come true!

COLONEL EILEEN M. COLLINS

United States Air Force

Preface

Since 1900, the world has become a completely different place. Life has changed for everyone—men, women, and even children. It's been especially true for women, as they struggled to lead independent lives. Women have fought for the right to vote, to own property, and to hold jobs. Led by a handful of brave pioneers, they have also worked to open the world of aviation to women. It was a battle that would take years to win.

In 1903, two men, Wilbur and Orville Wright, made history when they designed and successfully piloted a motorized airplane. Inspired by their example, other men soon took to the skies. No one wanted women to become pilots, however. With few exceptions, flying was reserved strictly for men.

During aviation's first years, airplanes were flimsy machines made of wire and heavy canvas fabric. Open cockpits had no seat belts or parachutes. Most aircraft were one of a kind. Men designed and built them as they went along. Accidents often happened. Men died at the rate of nearly one per day in airplane accidents. Fatal mistakes were brushed aside as just part of the game. When a woman pilot was killed in a crash, however, inferior intelligence or a lack of strength was listed as the cause. In fact, early aviation was a very dangerous activity for both men and women!

Most male pilots refused to teach women to fly. The few who were willing to provide lessons generally did so reluctantly. American aviation pioneers such as the Wright brothers and Glenn Curtiss didn't believe that women should learn to fly. Charles Lindbergh, the first person to make a solo flight across the Atlantic, was more liberal. He strongly supported his wife Anne's aviation ambitions, although he still didn't think that women belonged in military aviation. Newspaper articles questioned whether women were fit to fly. Editorials insisted that a woman's place was at home. Many doctors believed that women lacked physical energy. Still others thought women were likely to fall apart during emergencies.

Obtaining flight instruction was not just difficult; it was almost impossible for black women. Bessie Coleman was America's best-known pioneering, female, African-American aviator. Nevertheless, she had to go to France to take flying lessons, because no one in America would teach her. Two other African-American women, Willa Brown and Janet Bragg, overcame tremendous difficulties to promote aviation during the 1940s.

Even if a female would-be pilot could find a willing flight instructor, the cost was another problem. Most women lacked the money to fly. Flight lessons, not to mention airplanes, were expensive. By the 1940s, it cost approximately $700 to acquire a pilot's license. During the same period, the average woman earned less than $1,000 in an entire year. Men who could afford flight instruction weren't usually willing to pay for flying lessons for their wives or daughters.

Clothing was another issue. Several women had been killed when their long skirts were caught in the airplane's controls. Society, however, still thought trousers for women were scandalous. It didn't matter that the clothing was practical in the cockpit of an airplane. Trousers for women were improper, and that was all that mattered.

When aviation magazines wrote feature stories on women fliers, they focused more on fashion than on the women's aerial accomplishments. A *Sportsman Pilot* article titled "Flying Togs, Ancient and Modern" used several pages to describe the flying outfits of Katherine Stinson and Amelia Earhart. Ruth Law wore high leggings. Marjorie Stinson's normal flying uniform consisted of army pants worn with a boy's heavy white sweater. Harriet Quimby's plum-colored flying outfit received almost as much coverage as her skills as a pilot did.

Female airplane passengers also helped to convince the public that air travel was safe. On January 2, 1914, Mae Peabody of Dubuque, Iowa, became the first woman passenger on the world's first airline. The St. Petersburg-Tampa Airboat Line pilot was Tony Jannus, the famous Midwestern flier. He had also been the pilot in 1911 when Laura Merriam and Dorothy Williams flew as passengers in Washington, DC. Until that day, two women had never flown as passengers at the same time. In fact, only once before had two passengers in addition to the pilot flown at the same time in the United States. Both of them were men.

Like many women involved in aviation, Laura Merriam saw her flight as an adventure. She said, "I was not a bit scared when I made the flight and saw no reason to be." The following year, in 1912, Jannus also gave female aviator Katherine Stinson her first airplane ride in St. Louis. Just like most male pilots of the time, Jannus didn't object to women as airplane passengers, but he refused to teach them to fly.

The doors to aviation opened very slowly for women. By 1931, there were almost 16,000 licensed pilots in America. Fewer than 500 were women. Only thirty-nine women were certified as transport pilots. Most air races were restricted to men only. The first Women's Air Derby wasn't held until 1929. After the event, several of the fliers decided to start an organization for licensed female pilots. Ninety-nine women responded, giving the group its name—the Ninety-Nines. Its members still work toward expanded roles for women in aviation. Today dozens of other groups are also dedicated to the same goal.

Women Who Fly highlights the tremendous achievements made by American women in the world of aviation. They weren't alone, however. Women were also flying in other countries and overcoming similar obstacles. Harriet Quimby deserves credit as the first licensed American woman pilot. One year earlier, however, Baroness Raymonde de Laroche of France became the first woman in the world licensed to fly.

Since those early years, American women have continued to make aviation history. In 1932, Amelia Earhart made a solo crossing of the Atlantic Ocean. Thirty-two years later, Geraldine Mock became the first woman to fly alone around the world. Mock modestly described herself as a flying housewife, even though she set twenty-one speed and distance records during her flight. In 1986, Jeana A. Yeager served as copilot with Dick Rutan on a record-setting adventure. Their experimental aircraft, *Voyager*, became the first to fly around the world without stopping or refueling.

The National Aeronautics and Space Administration wanted to know if a woman could pass the same tests given to male astronaut candidates. A woman named Jerrie Cobb provided the answer. She passed the exams with flying colors. Sally Kristen Ride became the first American woman to go into space. Dr. Mae Jemison made history as the first African-American woman to enter NASA's astronaut program.

In January 1973, Frontier Airlines hired Emily Warner as a pilot. Three years later, she became the first female captain for a major American airline. Patrice Clarke Washington was the first black woman to accomplish the same feat. Barbara Allen Rainey made history as the first woman to wear naval aviator's wings. Betty Skelton, Patty Wagstaff, Jessie Woods, Evelyn "Bobbi" Trout, Laura Ingalls, Ruth Nichols—the list of female aviators and their achievements goes on and on.

Today women fly as private, aerobatic, commercial, and military pilots. They set records, win races, and break barriers as they pioneer new ground. They soar beyond the boundaries into outer space. For nearly a century, they have demonstrated the skills, determination, and courage of *Women Who Fly*.

PIONEERS

Chapter One

Pioneers

Most women didn't have careers in the early 1900s. A woman's job was to listen to her parents until she married and, after that, to obey her husband and take care of her children. Those women who had to work to support themselves or their families could choose from only a very few "suitable" jobs.

Fortunately, there were always exceptions to the rule—pioneers who went where no other woman had dared to go. Financial needs, a search for adventure, and a desire to do something different led these women to break the barriers society had set. In their footsteps, still other women follow.

America's earliest female fliers had several things in common. Harriet Quimby, Matilde Moisant, Blanche Stuart Scott, Julia Clark, Katherine Stinson, and Marjorie Stinson all wanted to fly. They were willing to do whatever it took to make that happen. Despite male disapproval, they believed they had a right to be pilots. They refused to take no for an answer.

Two women—Harriet Quimby and Matilde Moisant—made history less than eight years after the first flight of the Wright brothers. On August 1, 1911, Harriet Quimby became the first American woman to earn a pilot's license. Just twelve days later, Matilde Eleanor Moisant received her license. They had done something really special. Of the first one hundred licensed pilots in America, Harriet Quimby and Matilde Moisant were the only women.

Harriet Quimby set out with just one goal. She was determined to learn to fly, and no one was going to convince her otherwise. The young woman was often at the Moisant Aviation School—located at Garden City, Long Island, New York—before sunrise. When asked if she liked flying, she replied that she arrived at the field at four o'clock every morning. That ought to be enough of an answer.

Quimby wrecked one of the school's airplanes on May 4, 1911. During an attempted takeoff at full speed, the wheel fell off of the airplane's landing gear. The gear and one of the plane's wings were destroyed. Unhurt, Quimby quickly turned off the thirty-horsepower engine and jumped from the airplane.

Harriet Quimby failed in her first attempt to obtain her pilot's license, but she wasn't about to give up. The next morning, friends, newspaper reporters, fellow aviation students, and officials from the Aero Club of America watched her take the test again. Her airplane sped across the grass at Hempstead Plains and then lifted off the ground. At an altitude of 150 feet, Quimby efficiently performed the required tests. When she saw the applauding Aero Club of America observers, she realized she had passed her exam.

With her successful flight on August 1, 1911, Harriet Quimby entered the history books as the first American woman licensed to fly an airplane. She quickly became a celebrity. Thousands of people flocked to airshows to watch her fly.

On April 16, 1912, Harriet Quimby became the first woman to fly across the English Channel. In her job as an editor for *Leslie's Weekly,* Quimby had met many influential people in London. Those connections convinced the *London Mirror* to sponsor her flight from the English village of Dover to Calais on the French coast. In return, the newspaper received exclusive rights to her story.

For her flight, Quimby dressed in her usual satin-lined, thick-wool flying suit and two pairs of silk stockings. Knowing that it would be cold in the airplane's open cockpit, she wore a long woolen coat over her flying suit. On top of that, she wore a raincoat. The sky was clear but patches of heavy fog hid the French coast.

At 5:30 A.M., she took off. Crowds watched as she picked up altitude, flew over Dover Castle, and disappeared from sight. Soon she was flying above the English Channel. In the water below, photographers in the *Mirror*'s tugboat took just a few pictures. Then fog quickly enveloped Quimby's airplane. Dampness soaked her goggles and face. Unable to see or be seen, she flew on, using crude instruments, a compass, and her watch to plot her route.

Knowing she was flying at more than a mile per minute, Quimby judged that she had to be approaching land. She nosed the airplane down to an altitude of 1,000 feet, but there was still no sign of Calais. Bad weather and strong winds forced her to fly inland from the French coast. She saw a freshly plowed farmer's field that could possibly be used as a landing site but decided instead to set down on the beach. As the first woman to fly across the English Channel, Harriet Quimby became even more famous.

Months later, she was dead, the victim of a tragic accident. By the summer of 1912, Harriet Quimby was an experienced pilot. She now had hundreds of flights to her credit. At Squantum Field, south of Boston, Massachusetts, Quimby and her passenger, William A. P. Willard, were performing an exhibition. Unfortunately, they weren't wearing seat belts or parachutes. When the plane suddenly turned upside down, they fell to their deaths as thousands of spectators watched in horror.

Harriet Quimby had been more than America's first licensed female pilot. She was an accomplished photographer. She had also written hundreds of articles for *Leslie's Weekly* and several newspapers. Quimby was just twenty-eight years old.

While most men refused to teach women to fly, Alfred Moisant was an exception. When his flying school began offering lessons in April 1911, Harriet Quimby had been one of his first students. Spending much of her time at the Hempstead Plains airfield, Moisant's sister, Matilde, knew Blanche Stuart Scott, Harriet Quimby, and other women fliers. Just like them, Matilde wanted to fly.

For Matilde Moisant, getting her pilot's license involved following the same process as any other aviator. Every day, weather permitting, the instructor would allow her to fly for brief periods. Within a month,

Moisant was ready to try for her license. Her entire flying experience was a grand total of thirty-two minutes in the air. Twenty-three actual flights had lasted no more than a minute or two.

Moisant's test had been postponed twice because of bad weather. Now it finally took place. Several dozen friends offered encouragement. Dressed in her overalls, cap, and goggles, Moisant confidently took off in the school's *Lucky 13* airplane. She quickly performed the figure-eight maneuvers and the accurate landing test required by the Aero Club of America. Matilde Eleanor Moisant had just become America's second licensed woman pilot.

For the next few months, she worked to improve her skills. She flew as often as possible. On September 24, 1911, she competed against Harriet Quimby and French pilot Helene Dutrieu. When Moisant flew to an altitude of 1,200 feet, she won the Rodman-Wanamaker Trophy. During an air tour, she became one of the first women ever to fly in Mexico. As part of her brother's exhibition team, she performed at airshows across the country. Exhibition flying could be quite profitable, but Matilde Moisant flew more for fun than for money.

Moisant had decided that she would retire from flying after an exhibition at Wichita Falls, Texas, on April 14, 1912. After waiting all day for winds to subside, she took off at sunset. She quickly ascended to 2,500 feet, flew over the airfield for several minutes, and then prepared to land. Her plane hit the ground hard, bounced upward, and crashed down again. Flames enveloped the airplane. Several people pulled Moisant out, with her clothing ablaze. Thanks to their quick action, Matilde Moisant lived, but she never piloted an airplane again.

And then there was Blanche Stuart Scott—the first American woman to fly alone in an airplane. Scott started her career as an automobile driver, a daring job for a woman at that time. She made her first airplane flight on September 2, 1910. As she practiced taxiing up and down the field, her airplane suddenly rose forty feet into the air. The flight happened by accident, but Scott was still considered America's first woman to solo. Although she never obtained a pilot's license, she flew for exhibition teams at airshows throughout the United States.

Scott specialized in a "death dive," during which her airplane went into a steep descent from 4,000 feet. As the plane leveled out at an altitude of only 200 feet above the ground, spectators were scared and thrilled at the same time. Scott once commented that she felt people paid admission to airshows more to see potential fatal accidents than to see skilled fliers. Crowds just seemed to be fascinated by the possibility of injuries and even death. After only a few years of flying, Scott retired in 1916 at the age of twenty-seven. She'd had enough.

Julia Clark, the "Daring Girl Bird," became famous for the wrong reason. She was the first woman to graduate from the Curtiss Flying School in San Diego, California, and was also the third American woman licensed to fly. Unfortunately, she was also the first woman to die in an airplane crash in America. As a member of the Curtiss-Wright Aviators, Clark had been entertaining large crowds at airshows. On June 17, 1912, the daring fliers were set to perform at the Illinois State fairgrounds in Springfield. Julia Clark's flight would be the highlight.

In the air for only a few minutes, she performed the normal exhibition stunts. She flew the length of the course and did several lazy figure-eight tricks. At an altitude of only thirty feet above the ground, her airplane struck a small clump of trees and crashed. Clark was trapped in the wreckage. Too little experience and poor flying conditions had caused her death.

While Julia Clark might be criticized for flying in less-than-perfect conditions, airshow promoters expected pilots to fly regardless of the weather. Inexperience in the early 1900s wasn't limited to women pilots. The only way to learn was by doing. Aviation accidents were common for both male and female fliers. Julia Clark had been the third American woman licensed to fly. She was also the third woman to die while flying. Two other women, Denise Moore and Suzanne Bernard, were both killed in France.

Several members of the Stinson family were well known in the aviation world, but sisters Katherine and Marjorie achieved the greatest fame. Katherine was nicknamed the "Flying Schoolgirl." Her younger sister, Marjorie, was called the "Flying Schoolmarm."

Katherine Stinson's aviation career came about almost by accident. She really wanted to take singing and piano lessons but didn't have enough money for formal instruction. Then she read about the income pilots made at airshows. Stinson immediately sold her piano in order to pay for flying lessons. She figured that if she made enough money flying, she could afford her musical training.

Most women would-be fliers encountered frustration and male chauvinism. Stinson was no different. In the fall of 1911, she started lessons at a Kansas City flying school, but the school went out of business. The following January, she traveled to a flying school in St. Louis, operated by Thomas W. Benoist, owner of the Benoist Aeroplane Company. Stinson could not have found a better flying instructor than the one she found in Benoist's chief pilot, Tony Jannus. He was one of the best in the business in 1912, with thousands of flights to his credit. There was just one problem. Tony Jannus believed that women had no right to be in airplanes as anything other than passengers. Jannus took Stinson for a short flight but refused to give her lessons.

Not willing to give up, she approached the Mills School of Aviation in Chicago. Because of her small size and frail appearance, the school rejected her as a flying student. Stinson's experience was typical. Female fliers had to work twice as hard to prove they were as good as male pilots. Many men believed women did not have the brains, brawn, or courage to fly airplanes. Finally, at Cicero Field near Chicago, Stinson convinced Max Lillie to accept her as a flying student.

On July 24, 1912, Katherine Stinson earned the 196th license awarded by the Aero Club of America. That made her the fourth American woman licensed to fly. Stinson's life had changed. Music had been forgotten. Flying was everything. She spent the rest of the summer and fall flying at Chicago and St. Louis. Then she headed to Hot Springs, Arkansas, to spend the winter with her family. The following May, she started the Stinson Aviation Company, to control all of her exhibition-flying activities. Katherine Stinson became president. Her mother, Emma, served as secretary and treasurer.

In June, she bought her first airplane, a Wright Model B. She also hired William Pickens as her manager. In mid-July, she agreed to fly at Coney Island Park in Cincinnati, Ohio. A month later, Stinson was flying at Columbus, Indiana. On September 1, 1913, she flew as part of a Labor Day celebration in Pine Bluff, Arkansas.

At the Montana State Fair, Stinson flew several exhibitions each day. Passengers paid to fly with her. She became the first woman flier to carry mail by air when she took postcards and letters from the fairgrounds to the federal building in Helena. The Illinois State Fair at Springfield was her next exhibition stop. When Katherine Stinson flew a three-day engagement in El Paso, Texas, in late October, people there saw a female pilot for the first time.

She performed everywhere, flying nearly every week. An exhibition at Helena, Arkansas, followed her show at El Paso. Then she was in Phoenix, Arizona, and Beaumont, Texas. Katherine Stinson provided aerial entertainment at a Tulane University football game in New Orleans, Louisiana. Most of the winter was spent in Texas, while mechanics overhauled her well-worn plane. Meanwhile she practiced her flying at airshows around the state.

After the exhibition season began in early spring, Stinson spent 1914 flying at the same frenzied pace. At Kansas City's Overland Park in August, an exciting event took place. Her sister Marjorie had recently graduated from the Wright brothers' flying school at Dayton, Ohio. Now, for the first time, the two sisters flew together. On another occasion, Katherine Stinson ran out of gas during one of her flights. She landed safely in a vineyard where friendly farmers refueled the plane's tank, and she continued flying. As part of her act in Fresno, California, she flew over the fairgrounds at night while a searchlight illuminated her airplane.

For most of the winter of 1914 and spring of 1915, the Stinson family gathered in San Antonio, Texas. Brothers Edward and Jack served as mechanics for the sisters, while Katherine and Marjorie taught them to fly. During the winter months, both young women did everything they could to promote aviation. In their new hometown, they lectured at schools, businesses, and civic organizations.

Lincoln Beachey had been the greatest daredevil stunt pilot of aviation's early years. When he died in a crash, Katherine Stinson bought the eighty-horsepower engine that had powered his airplane. She then hired his mechanic to install the engine in an airplane that she was having built. Stinson received her new plane on July 12, 1915. Six days later, the "Flying Schoolgirl" did something no other woman had ever done. She performed the loop-the-loop. The trick quickly became part of her act.

In December Katherine Stinson performed yet another first for a woman flier. Flying over the city of Los Angeles, California, she attached several magnesium flares to her airplane. Looping the loop through the night sky, she spelled out "C-A-L" in the darkness. Two months later, on February 16, 1916, she treated Chicago to the same trick. In a combined day and night show, she looped the loop and lit up the sky with her aerial fireworks. The remainder of 1916 was equally busy, but there was more to come.

In mid-December 1916, Katherine Stinson and her airplane sailed from San Francisco to Japan. Huge crowds turned out to see the first woman to fly in Japan. On one flight over Tokyo, 25,000 Japanese watched her loop the loop. In mid-February, Stinson visited China, where Li Yüan-hung, the president of China, called her the "Granddaughter of Heaven."

When America entered World War I, Katherine Stinson offered her flying services to the Signal Corps of the United States Army. The military wasn't ready to accept women pilots and turned her down. Still wanting to do her part for her country, she drove ambulances in France. On behalf of the American Red Cross, she made exhibition flights that raised thousands of dollars for the war effort.

Ill health led Katherine Stinson to stop flying in the early 1920s. When she married Miguel Otero, Jr., a World War I aviator, in 1928, they promised each other that they would never fly again. In July 1977, at the age of eighty-six, Katherine Stinson, the world-renowned pioneer aviator and stunt flier, died. Her husband died just months later.

When Katherine Stinson's sister Marjorie wanted to learn to fly, Katherine had refused to teach her. She feared that Marjorie would be hurt. After all, the odds of long life for aviators, especially women, weren't good. Katherine Stinson had been the fourth American woman licensed to fly. Of the first three, Harriet Quimby and Julia Clark had both died in crashes, and Matilde Moisant was no longer flying.

After Katherine's refusal, Marjorie entered the Wright brothers' flying school at Dayton, Ohio, in mid-June 1914. Her flying class included Lieutenant Kenneth Whiting of the United States Navy as well as one student from Japan and another from England. Contrary to his usual misgivings about teaching women to fly, Orville Wright personally took Marjorie out to the flying field and introduced her to her instructor. Howard Rinehart was a tough teacher who frequently yelled at his students when they made a mistake. Marjorie Stinson became a frequent target, not just because she was a woman and the youngest student, but also because she had foolishly told a reporter that she expected to qualify for her license in only six weeks.

Marjorie Stinson, not yet eighteen and the youngest woman pilot in America, received license number 303 on August 8, 1914. She wrote ". . . six weeks to the day. At last I have my pilot's license, after flying instruction totaling 4½ hours!" *Flight* magazine reported, "Following the example of her sister, Miss Katherine Stinson, who has been flying a Wright biplane for a long time in various parts of the States, Miss Marjorie Stinson has just qualified as pilot at the Wright School at Dayton. She is now going to Chicago in order to fly her sister's Wright at the Cicero Aerodrome of the Aero Club of Illinois."

Within days, Marjorie Stinson entered the airshow circuit full time with her first public exhibition flight at Overland Park, Kansas City, Missouri. In early October, thousands of visitors turned out at the Free Fall Fair in Brownwood, Texas, to watch Marjorie fly. A local newspaper reported that "cheer after cheer was sounded as she soared away into the sky as if with the wings of a bird." Flying over the courthouse, she executed a spectacular figure eight to the delight of the onlookers. Her thirty-five-minute flight almost ended in an accident. Hit by strong winds, her airplane shot upward, then just as suddenly was pushed toward the ground. After the near tragedy, Marjorie Stinson recalled, "It was the first time in my life that I was afraid. I began wondering whether I would fall in the creek, or in a tree, and wondered whether all my bones would be broken."

In May 1915, Albert Bond Lambert appointed Marjorie as the first female member of the United States Aviation Reserve Corps. That year also saw a new career for Marjorie, with the establishment of the Stinson School of Flying at San Antonio. The weather in that part of Texas was ideal for flying. The 750-acre field was described as absolutely level, hard, and smooth, with few obstructions. It included a first-class machine shop and a hangar large enough to house four airplanes. *Aerial Age Weekly* described Marjorie Stinson as "a little girl, still in her teens, yet she is teaching big brawny fellows the art of flying and converting them into enthusiastic airmen."

Stinson began teaching Canadian flight students almost by accident. Four Canadian men asked if she would teach them to fly. In spite of hardly any teaching experience, Stinson agreed. Her method of instruction combined theory and hands-on flying. She ended her first lecture to her students with "a promise to permit each man to assume as much control of the plane as he could safely handle. And I promised to ground anyone who did not release all control at a given signal from me and allow me to land the plane in case of trouble." To decide which student would take the first flight, she flipped a coin.

Business was good. The Canadians were happy with Stinson's method of instruction. Before her first four students had soloed, she had another ten Canadian hopefuls at the school. At one point, Stinson had sixteen students in her class. She was flying as much as six hours a day, making short flights that translated into hundreds of takeoffs and landings. She was on her way to becoming known as the "Flying Schoolmarm."

With the war in Europe raging, the Canadian government wanted pilots trained as quickly as possible. Stinson obliged them. For Stinson, graduating flight students meant a sense of accomplishment as well as a feeling of dread. She knew all of her Canadian students would soon be facing danger as they flew under wartime conditions in Europe.

Stinson's main objective was to teach fliers for the military, but she did not hesitate to also teach civilians, male and female. John Frost, a resident of San Antonio, was the first "private" student to graduate from the Stinson School of Flying. Regarding female pilots, Marjorie said, "Much has been said about whether or not women should actually pilot their own planes. As I see it, there is no question about it. Women have been flying successfully for years."

While still operating the aviation school, Marjorie Stinson continued to fly frequent exhibitions throughout the United States. One of her most popular acts included a bombing attack on a mock battleship. In May 1919, when both Stinson sisters flew at the Pan American Aeronautical Exposition in Atlantic City, New Jersey, Marjorie won a trophy.

Although overshadowed by her more famous sister, Katherine, Marjorie's accomplishments were second to none. Before she was twenty years old, the "Flying Schoolmarm" had helped to train more than one hundred American and Canadian student pilots for World War I.

The Stinson School of Flying operated for several years before closing in 1918. Marjorie Stinson's flying career ended when she moved to Washington, DC, the following year. There she became a draftsman, first with the U.S. Navy and later at the War Department. When she died on April 15, 1975, at the age of seventy-nine, her body was cremated. Airmailed to San Antonio, Texas, Marjorie Stinson's ashes were strewn over Stinson Field from a 1931 Curtiss airplane.

EARLY BIRDS

Chapter Two

Early Birds

Ruth Law did it all. She was an airmail pilot, skilled aerobatic flier, and businesswoman. Known as "Angel Ruth," the "Lady Daredevil," and the "Queen of the Air," she flew all over the world. In the years between 1912 and 1922, Ruth Law was one of America's best-known female pilots.

Her introduction to flying was typical. Orville Wright refused to teach her to fly, but he was still willing to sell her a Wright Model B biplane. Had he realized that Law was married, Wright would have been even more difficult. A well-reasoned argument could sometimes convince male aviators to teach a woman to fly, but few men were willing to provide flight instruction for a married woman.

After Wright's rejection, Ruth Law took her first airplane flight on July 5, 1912, at the Burgess Flying School near Boston, Massachusetts. Less than a month later, she soloed. She flew as often as possible. By November 1912, Law had earned license number 188. Her husband, Charles Oliver, served as her manager and agent.

On January 12, 1913, Ruth Law made history before a crowd of 5,000 people. On that warm Sunday afternoon in Daytona Beach, she became the first woman to pilot an airplane in Florida. Two years later, *Billboard* called Law "the only sensational lady aviator doing the 'spiral dive,' 'dip of death,' 'steep banking' and many other thrillers more dangerous than the loop." After such nerve-wracking exhibition flying, the daring pilot relaxed by doing embroidery.

On the morning of November 20, 1916, Chicago's weather was cold and gray. It was a good day to spend indoors sitting next to a warm fire. Ruth Law had other plans, however. She intended to fly nonstop from Chicago to New York. In the process, she would set a new American cross-country record. Although she was an experienced pilot who had been flying for several years, Law had never flown any distance greater than twenty-five miles. A trip of almost 900 miles was a tremendous undertaking for anyone—man or woman.

Dressed for the cold temperatures, she wore the standard flying outfit of wool and leather. One magazine described her as looking like "a young Eskimo in his Sunday clothes." Mechanics loaded as much fuel as possible onto Law's Curtiss airplane. The engine roared in the cold air as the plane rolled across the brown sod of Grant Park. Enthusiastic spectators who had been waiting since before sunrise cheered as Law's airplane slowly lifted off the ground at 8:25 A.M.

After taking off, she hugged the coast of Lake Michigan as she flew toward Gary, Indiana. The almost thirty-mile-per-hour wind blowing off the lake soon dropped, but the tail wind she had hoped for never materialized. For much of the trip, Law kept her altitude at around 1,000 feet. That made it easier to follow railroad tracks and search for landmarks. Near Cleveland, Ohio, she ascended to an altitude of 6,000 feet. Over Erie, Pennsylvania, she was at 3,000 feet. Passing Olean, New York, Law headed due east.

After flying 590 miles in five hours and forty-five minutes, she was running low on gas. She was forced to land at Hornell to refuel. Two weeks earlier, a man named Victor Carlstrom had set the American cross-country nonstop record. Although Law hadn't yet reached her final destination of New York City, she had bettered that record by 138 miles. Barely an hour later, Law's small plane left for the next stop, ninety miles away. Heavy fog forced her to fly level with the treetops, a dangerous tactic in the hilly regions of New York. At 4:20 P.M., Law landed at Binghamton. She had covered 680 miles. It was too late to go any further that day.

Leaving Binghamton the next morning, she immediately ran into strong winds and thick fog. Again, she had to fly as low to the ground as possible, navigating up and down hills as if on a roller coaster. Flying over lakes and mountains, Law finally reached the Hudson River. Dropping low over the water, she knew her trip was almost over.

As Law neared New York City, her airplane's engine began to sputter. Her supply of gasoline was running low. Within minutes, her plane made a long glide onto the parade ground of Governor's Island, just off the southern end of Manhattan. Hundreds of well-wishers cheered as the half-frozen Law climbed from the aircraft and stripped off her gloves and leather flying helmet. She began to walk around, trying to get some warmth back into her body. Her face was blue from the icy temperatures and fierce winds. All she could say was "I'm cold." In an automobile headed to the quarters of Major Carl F. Hartmann, commander of Governor's Island, Law borrowed Mrs. Hartmann's powder puff and redid her makeup.

Ruth Law had made the trip from Chicago to New York City in eight hours, fifty-five minutes, and thirty-five seconds of flying time. She had set a new American distance record of 884 miles. Her only regret was that she hadn't been able to make the entire flight nonstop. Before her trip, she had tried to convince Glenn Curtiss to sell her a larger airplane that could carry more fuel, but Curtiss turned her down. She recalled, "He wouldn't let me have it, because he said 'the big machine was too much for a girl to handle.'"

Only a few weeks later, on December 2, 1916, Law gave a nighttime flying exhibition in New York to celebrate the installation of floodlights around the Statue of Liberty. A mixture of small boats and larger ships filled the harbor for the occasion. Ferryboats carried thousands of people. The U.S. Navy's Atlantic fleet proudly displayed their red, white, and blue colors.

At six o'clock, President Woodrow Wilson pulled a switch aboard the presidential yacht *Mayflower*. Instantly, bright white lights illuminated the Statue of Liberty. Whistles from hundreds of boats screamed into the night. Naval vessels fired off booming twenty-one-gun salutes. Fireworks burst over the harbor. Red flares lit up the shoreline.

Suddenly, out of nowhere, a flash of flame erupted high above Lady Liberty. It was Ruth Law in her Curtiss biplane. Golden sparks and red streams of fire seemed to spout from the tail and wings of her airplane as she circled the southern tip of Manhattan. Thousands of excited

spectators cheered as electric lights on the bottom of Law's plane out-
lined the word *liberty*. It was quite an event.

Two weeks later, the Aero Club of America and the Civil Forum
held a dinner in Ruth Law's honor at the Hotel Astor. Four hundred
people watched as the Aero Club of America presented her with a
$2,500 check for her record-setting long-distance flight. Admiral
Robert E. Peary, discoverer of the North Pole, told the audience that
Law's "splendid accomplishment has shone so that the whole world
may read what a woman can do."

Her accomplishment wasn't enough, however, to change attitudes
in the military. When America entered World War I in 1917, Ruth Law
tried to enlist in the U.S. Army. It was a battle she had no chance of
winning. The government had decided not to accept women as commissioned officers or in the enlisted ranks. After the war, Law expanded her aviation career, flying not just in America but also in Japan,
China, and the Philippines. For carrying the first official airmail in the
Philippines, she received the Philippine Aero Club Medal.

Several factors led to her decision to retire from flying in 1922. She
had been flying for ten years. That was a long time in the dangerous
early days of American aviation. Exhibition flying could be financial-
ly rewarding, but it was a risky way to make a living. Fair managers
and promoters demanded increasingly aggressive stunts. Perhaps most
significantly, Ruth Law explained, "My husband worried so much that
he finally had a nervous breakdown. I felt that since he had allowed
me ten years of the sport, I owed it to him to give it up."

Stunts Ruth Law had performed at an airshow in 1919 convinced
Phoebe Fairgrave to fly. Her biggest challenge was to find an instructor. Hoping to make her give up any idea of flying, the pilot on
Phoebe's first flight performed a series of loops and dives to frighten
her. His strategy backfired. Fairgrave loved the aerobatics. The next
day, she returned to the airfield and bought a war-surplus Curtiss JN-
4D airplane, but she still had no one to teach her to fly it. Fortunately,
she came across Vernon Omlie. He was an enlightened young man
who was willing to accept her as a flight student.

After just a few lessons, Vernon Omlie quit his job as a flight instructor and went to work for Phoebe Fairgrave. Together they embarked on an aggressive campaign of exhibition flying at fairs throughout the United States. As if flying wasn't enough, Fairgrave soon took up a new activity—parachute jumping. Eighteen years old and one year out of high school, she stood just over five feet in height and weighed only ninety-six pounds. Phoebe, however, was fearless.

On July 10, 1921, at St. Paul, Minnesota, Phoebe Fairgrave set the world's altitude record in parachute jumping for women. Just before her jump, a newspaperman asked permission to photograph her as she sat in the cockpit of her Curtiss airplane. Obligingly, she said, "I suppose you want me to smile. It may be the last time I shall laugh." In case of an unexpected water landing, she wore an inflated automobile inner tube around her waist.

After taking off, the pilot took Fairgrave's bright-red Curtiss airplane to an altitude of 15,200 feet. Phoebe climbed out of the open cockpit and crouched on the bottom wing. Suddenly, she leaped in the air and dropped like a rock for 5,000 feet before the parachute finally opened. As the white muslin sheets of her parachute billowed above her head, she slowly fell to the ground. When her feet finally touched the earth below, she owned a new altitude record for female parachutists.

From 1921 to 1925, Phoebe Fairgrave and Vernon Omlie continued exhibition flying. When the couple met Glenn Messer, another exhibition flier, they teamed up to operate the Phoebe Fairgrave-Glenn Messer Flying Circus. Phoebe jumped out of airplanes and, in a display of total fearlessness, performed death-defying wing-walking acts. She also flew aerial stunts for the *Perils of Pauline* movies, produced by the Fox Moving Picture Company.

When Phoebe Fairgrave and Vernon Omlie married in 1922, the time had come for them to settle down. Memphis, Tennessee, seemed like the perfect place. They founded an aviation school that was credited as the first commercial school in the mid-South. There they offered flight instruction, carried passengers, and continued their exhibition flying.

After the Omlies helped to start the Memphis Aero Club in 1925, the next logical step was the formation of their own airline. Named

Mid-South Airways, the company's first route was Memphis to Chicago. When the airline made its inaugural flight on May 7, 1928, Percy McDonald, the first passenger, paid sixty dollars for a round-trip flight from Memphis to Chicago. The airline had a brief but successful life until the Great Depression caused business to dry up.

In June 1927, Phoebe Fairgrave Omlie became the first woman to receive a transport pilot's license (number 199) and an airplane mechanic's license (number 423) from the Department of Commerce. The transport pilot's license required a minimum of 200 flight hours. It permitted the holder to engage in interstate aerial commerce and to pilot any type of airplane. No other woman had made such an accomplishment.

On June 29, 1929, Phoebe Fairgrave Omlie narrowly avoided disaster while making history. When she flew a Monocoupe to an altitude of 25,400 feet above the airport at Moline, Illinois, she broke two aviation records previously held by Louise McPhetridge von Thaden and Barney Zimmerling.

At 3:30 P.M., the maintenance crew wheeled her airplane onto the flight line and loaded oxygen tanks on board. Omlie climbed into the airplane's cockpit and began warming up the engine while she went through her preflight check. An official from the National Aeronautical Association stowed in the airplane's cabin a sealed barograph to record altitude.

Minutes later, Phoebe headed her airplane down the runway and began her climb. At 19,000 feet, she slipped an oxygen mask onto her face and turned on the oxygen tanks. The higher she went, the colder it got. The temperature was barely above zero at 24,000 feet. Fortunately, she wore plenty of warm clothing. Everything looked good.

At 25,400 feet, her engine blew a spark plug. An oil line broke, spraying hot oil into her face. Blinded by the oil and suffering from insufficient oxygen, she quickly pushed down on the controls, dropping the airplane's nose. Feeling groggy, dizzy, and barely able to see, she brought her Monocoupe in for a landing. The flight had taken two hours and five minutes.

That same year, she won the Women's Air Derby from Santa Monica, California, to Cleveland, Ohio. In 1930 she won the Eastern

Derby, an aerial race from Washington, DC, to Chicago. The following year, she again took first place in the Santa Monica to Cleveland race.

In 1934, Omlie planned and directed a national air-marking program for the Bureau of Air Commerce. Under the plan, black and orange directional signs were painted on the roofs of buildings as navigational aides for pilots. As part of her job, Phoebe studied flying conditions at the nation's aviation facilities. In just one month, she logged over 5,000 miles while visiting twenty airports in eleven states.

Omlie hired several of America's most experienced and well-known women pilots to work for her. Louise von Thaden, Nancy Harkness Love, Helen Richey, and Blanche Noyes were her assistants. As the air-marking program continued throughout 1935, Eleanor Roosevelt named Phoebe Fairgrave Omlie one of the nation's ten most outstanding women for her contributions to American aviation.

Her air-marking program had been a tremendous success. Under Phoebe Omlie's direction, 16,000 air markers were constructed throughout the United States. Her crew of fliers proved that women were more than capable of such projects. Unfortunately, World War II led to the destruction of her department's hard work. Fearing that the directional signs would benefit enemy attackers, the War Department ordered that the air markers be dismantled.

The end of her air-marking program didn't mean the end of Phoebe Omlie's involvement in aviation. When her husband was killed in a plane crash at St. Louis in 1936, she gave up her position as special assistant for air intelligence and returned to Tennessee. The following year, she and Percy McDonald set up the nation's first public-school vocational course in aviation. Phoebe Omlie was a firm believer in aviation education. She spent her remaining years encouraging young men and women to enter the world of flight.

Evelyn Trout began flying a few years after Ruth Law and Phoebe Omlie. Born in 1906 in Illinois, she spent her early years moving from town to town. Nicknamed "Bobbi" for her short "bobbed" hairstyle, Trout didn't care for typical, girlish kinds of things. In high school, she wanted to take classes in mechanics, not home economics. She talked her parents into buying a gas station for her to run. It was so successful that her father eventually quit his job and went to work for her.

Trout originally wanted to be either a cowgirl or a motorcycle racer. A ride in a Curtiss Jenny airplane when she was just sixteen changed all that. She wanted to learn to fly instead. With the money she made at the service station to pay for lessons, she was on her way to the record books.

By 1928, Bobbi Trout was already well known to aviation fans. In fact, Walt Disney hired her because of her fame. With a plane filled with Mickey Mouse dolls, Trout provided exciting publicity for the new Disney character.

The following year, she set her first endurance record. On January 2, 1929, she kept her plane in the air for twelve hours and eleven minutes. At the end of the month, another female aviator named Elinor Smith added one hour to that time. Two weeks later, Bobbi Trout took back the record by flying without stopping for seventeen hours and five minutes. In the process, she also became the first woman to fly all night!

In June she set a new women's altitude record of 15,200 feet. In August, Trout was one of nineteen participants in the first Women's Air Derby. She managed to complete the California-to-Ohio race despite several mishaps. All of her mechanical experience came in handy. On one occasion, she repaired her airplane with some wire and scrap metal she managed to find.

In November, Bobbi Trout and Elinor Smith combined their efforts. They set a new endurance record of just over forty-two hours. On January 1, 1931, Trout and fellow flier Edna May celebrated the New Year by setting another record. Their airplane stayed aloft for more than 122 hours.

Bobbi Trout was the fifth woman to earn her license as a transport pilot. When she wasn't competing in air races and setting records, Bobbi Trout also taught others to fly and worked as a commercial photographer. During World War II, she performed aerial surveillance for the Los Angeles Police Department. During the war, Trout once again put her mechanical skills to work when she invented a machine to sort scrap aircraft rivets.

Trout made the news again more than fifty years later. On January 1, 1929, she had received her international pilot's license, signed by Orville Wright, president of the Fédération Aéronautique Internationale. On February 3, 1995, the first woman to pilot a Space Shuttle, Eileen Collins, carried Trout's license with her into space. It was a fitting tribute to all female aviation pioneers. Bobbi Trout died on January 24, 2003, at the age of ninety-seven.

CROSSING OCEANS

Chapter Three

Crossing Oceans

If it was hard for women to find someone to teach them to fly during the early years of aviation, it was almost impossible for African-Americans. Sheer determination enabled Bessie Coleman to become the first African-American, male or female, licensed to fly an airplane. Ever since the Wright brothers' first flight, almost every pilot had dreamed of being the first to make a solo transatlantic crossing. When Bessie Coleman crossed the ocean, however, it wasn't by air. She had no choice; she went by ship. No one in America would teach her to fly. She was forced to go to Europe in order to receive flight instruction.

Born on January 26, 1892, Bessie Coleman's early life had been filled with frustration and poverty. As a young girl in Texas, she picked cotton to help support her family. At the age of twenty-seven, she went to work as a beautician in Chicago. Then she decided that she wanted to learn to fly.

Coleman faced major obstacles. First of all, she had no money to pay for flying lessons. Besides that, even if she had the financial means, she had no one to teach her. Few white men would provide flight instruction for a black man, let alone a black woman. The fact that there was only a handful of African-American pilots in the United States made it even more difficult.

In Chicago, Bessie Coleman met Robert Abbott, editor and publisher of the *Chicago Defender,* one of the country's largest African-American newspapers. Abbott suggested that Coleman take flying lessons in France, where there might be less prejudice against both women and blacks. Bessie Coleman didn't have the funds to go to Europe. She also didn't speak French. Undaunted, she began taking language lessons and saving her money.

In November 1920, Bessie Coleman went to France but found that no one there was interested in giving her flying lessons. Finally, she convinced Rene and Gaston Caudron to take her on as a student. On June 15, 1921, Bessie Coleman, a black woman, earned her pilot's license. She had accomplished something no other African-American had ever done.

Despite additional flight training in France the following spring, she still had little flying experience. Nevertheless, the *Chicago Defender* called her the "world's greatest woman flier." When Coleman flew at Glenn Curtiss Field in New York, before a mostly black audience, the *Call* of Kansas City touted "the first public flight of a black woman" in the United States.

Continuing financial difficulties kept her from flying as often as she would have liked. The airplanes she used were frequently old and in poor condition. Accidents and periods of long inactivity hurt her flying career. A crash while flying at Santa Monica, California, in 1923 left her with fractured ribs and a broken leg that took several months to heal. During the next two years, she spent little time in the air.

Nicknamed "Queen Bess," Coleman returned to flying with a vengeance in the summer of 1925. Using borrowed or rented airplanes, she appeared before both black and white crowds throughout Texas. In the fall, she returned to Chicago and took to the lecture circuit. She wanted to earn enough money to buy her own airplane and open a flying school for African-Americans. In January 1926, Bessie Coleman left Chicago to lecture in the Georgia cities of Savannah, Augusta, and Atlanta. In February, she was in Florida, speaking at black theaters and churches. From St. Petersburg and Tampa, she headed to Orlando, then to West Palm Beach.

By April 1926, Bessie Coleman's tour had reached Jacksonville, Florida. On May 1, she was scheduled to be the main event of a flying exhibition at the annual Negro Welfare League Field Day. She also planned to make a parachute jump using her own airplane—a well-worn Curtiss Jenny that she had just purchased.

April 30, 1926, was a typical warm spring day in Jacksonville. Bessie Coleman and William Wills decided to test-fly her new airplane and check out the field in preparation for the airshow the next day. Wills, a white mechanic, was at the controls in the front seat. Bessie Coleman sat in the rear. Neither wore a seat belt.

Wills took off and flew the Curtiss Jenny to an altitude of nearly 4,000 feet. As they headed back to the airfield, the nose of the airplane suddenly dipped. Within seconds the out-of-control airplane spun downward. At an altitude of 500 feet, the airplane flipped upside down. Coleman was thrown to the ground. William Wills died at the controls as the plane crashed. Bessie Coleman, the first licensed African-American aviator, was dead at the age of thirty-four.

Bessie Coleman had fought overwhelming obstacles to realize her dream of becoming a pilot. Although she was never able to fulfill her goal of opening a flying school for African-Americans, she did something far more important. She introduced black audiences to the field of aviation. At the same time, she proved that African-Americans were every bit as capable of flying as whites.

Excited by Charles Lindbergh's successful flight, pilots wanted to fly across the Atlantic Ocean more than ever. Ruth Elder almost made it. She came so close to being the first woman to successfully cross the Atlantic Ocean by air. Instead, she had to settle for being the first woman to attempt a transatlantic flight.

Elder picked a man from her hometown of Lakeland, Florida, as her copilot and flight instructor. She also wisely chose someone who knew his way around an airplane. Flying since 1917, George Haldeman shared Elder's desire to fly across the Atlantic. Equally important, he was able to raise the money to fund the very expensive project. With the financial help of Edward Cornell, a wealthy Florida citrus-grove owner; Thomas H. McArdle, a real-estate salesman; and a group of well-to-do West Virginia businessmen, Haldeman was able to buy an airplane and pay for its modification.

Flying was never an easy proposition for a woman, especially one with a husband. When the project's investors learned that Miss Ruth

Elder was really Mrs. Lyle Womack, they demanded that her husband sign the contract. They wanted his permission for her to make the flight. Discovering that the businessman was in Panama, they decided to keep Elder's marriage a secret.

In late August 1927, George Haldeman and Ruth Elder flew from Lakeland to Detroit to test a Stinson Detroiter, the airplane they intended to use to make their transatlantic flight. Afterward Elder piloted Haldeman's Waco monoplane back to Tampa, Florida, making the 1,100-mile nonstop flight in slightly less than twelve hours. Woefully short of flying experience, she had fewer than 200 hours in her logbook. She needed all the time in the air that she could get.

In preparation for their flight, Elder and Haldeman spent several hundred hours flying their airplane under the same conditions that they would experience over the ocean. First Haldeman outfitted the Stinson with the finest equipment available. Then he hired a pair of airmail pilots to teach them how to fly using instruments. When their backers tried to convince Elder and Haldeman to delay their Atlantic crossing for at least a year and enter the New York-Spokane Aerial Derby instead, Elder and Haldeman rejected the suggestion. Elder said, "We agreed to go and are going."

Satisfied that their flying skills were up to the task, Elder and Haldeman left Florida for New York's Roosevelt Field on September 14 to begin their flight. Only months after Charles Lindbergh's history-making conquest of the Atlantic Ocean, the unthinkable was about to happen. A woman was going to do the same thing! Overwhelming press coverage dubbed Ruth Elder "the American Girl." Their bright-orange airplane was christened *American Girl*. Elder told reporters, "The plane is in perfect condition and the weather will not bother us much. We expect to take off Sunday and land in Paris without incident." The words would come back to haunt her.

A problem arose. Ruth Elder did not have her private pilot's license, a basic requirement. She was supposed to take her test on September 17 but didn't show up. The next day, she took only the flight physical exam. Finally, on the afternoon of September 19, Elder received her coveted pilot's license.

Elder and Haldeman intended to travel south of the route taken by Charles Lindbergh. By following the shipping lanes, they could receive current weather reports from the ships. They also wanted the ships to watch for them in case they experienced trouble en route. The pair hoped to leave for Europe immediately, but bad weather over the Atlantic Ocean delayed their takeoff. Elder met with reporters and shopped in New York City. Haldeman and his team of mechanics worked on the airplane.

Elder was worried that Frances Grayson, another woman planning to cross the Atlantic, would beat her to the punch. On September 22, Elder announced that she would start her trip the following day. September 23 came and went as bad weather continued to hold them back. All that was left to do was to fuel the airplane, but *American Girl* remained in the hangar at Roosevelt Field. Elder seemed about to give up. She gave herself until October 15. If the weather over the Atlantic Ocean didn't clear by then, the flight would have to be postponed.

On the morning of October 11, Haldeman received the best weather report in weeks. He declared, "It's now or never." James Kimball of the Weather Bureau expressed his confidence in Haldeman's skills. When their backers tried to talk the fliers out of going, Elder left the final decision to the more experienced Haldeman.

Mechanics fueled the aircraft. Roast-chicken sandwiches and thermos bottles full of coffee were put on board. Haldeman made last-minute adjustments to the airplane's engine. Elder posed for photographers. The *Lakeland Evening Ledger* reported, "The twenty-three-year-old pilot cut a fancy figure in her flight suit over checked golf knickers, checked stockings, and two-tone shoes."

Fully loaded, the airplane weighed 5,600 pounds, almost 400 pounds more than Lindbergh's *Spirit of St. Louis*. The 520 gallons of gas on board *American Girl* would allow a nonstop flight of 4,000 miles. Haldeman kissed his wife goodbye, Elder threw a kiss to crowds surrounding the airplane, and the fliers climbed into the cockpit. At the end of the runway, virtually the same spot from which Lindbergh had started five months earlier, Haldeman said, "We'll make it all right." Elder agreed, "Sure, we will."

A successful Atlantic crossing by the two pilots would mark the first flight across the Atlantic by an American woman. It would also be the longest nonstop over-water flight ever taken. As Haldeman gave the plane full throttle, *American Girl* lifted off the runway at Roosevelt Field at 5:04 P.M. on October 11, 1927, headed for Paris. The weather forecast had been worse than Haldeman had revealed. They were headed into less-than-desirable weather. The flight would take thirty-eight to forty-two hours. There would be two pitch-black nights of instrument flying.

Ships along the route reported frequent sightings of *American Girl.* A freighter saw them approximately 600 miles from New York. They were spotted again 120 miles later. Two hours after that, another ship reported seeing them. *American Girl* appeared to be on track. Thousands of people gathered in Paris at Le Bourget Airport in anticipation of their triumphant arrival. Then, for the next twenty-eight hours, no one saw the aircraft. It might have been forced off course. Even worse, it might have gone down in the ocean. No one knew.

Aboard *American Girl,* exhaustion had taken its toll on the fliers. At one point, Elder slept solidly for two hours until Haldeman awakened her. He needed her to keep him awake by constantly thumping him on the back. With Elder at the controls a while later, Haldeman crawled to the back of the airplane to pour fuel into the main tank. Heavy turbulence made it difficult for Elder to keep the airplane's nose up, so Haldeman took control while Elder fueled the tank. As she lay on her side, struggling to lift thirty-pound fuel cans in the dark, Elder spilled gasoline in the cabin. Fumes quickly made the fliers dizzy and sick to their stomachs.

Fatigue wasn't their only problem. Despite flying at different altitudes, they couldn't escape fierce storms that made their position uncertain. Heavy sleet froze on the airplane's control and wing surfaces. They were forced to throw some of their fuel overboard to reduce weight. Elder and Haldeman were in trouble but had no choice except to fly on. They might not have enough fuel to reach Paris. Perhaps, they could make it to Spain.

American Girl developed an oil leak. As the oil pressure dropped, their speed slowed from 120 to only 70 miles per hour. Flying over a

Dutch tanker, the SS *Barendrecht,* the pilots dropped a message, "How far are we from land and which way?" Crewmen painted the answer on the ship's deck: "True S, 40 W, 360 miles Terceira, Azores." Land was nearly four hundred miles away. They couldn't last that long. With so much gasoline still on board, a crash might cause a fire. Elder and Haldeman circled the ship for nearly an hour using up fuel. They knew that they would have to land in the ocean.

The ship's captain stopped his engines and a crew lowered a lifeboat as *American Girl* hit the water in a perfect landing. As their airplane bobbed up and down in the Atlantic Ocean, their flight ended in defeat. Elder and Haldeman climbed onto one of the plane's wings and waved as they waited for the sailors to reach them. Minutes later, Elder and Haldeman were aboard the ship. A radio message sent to the Paris office of the Associated Press read, "Landed by SS *Barendrecht* with broken oil line. Both Haldeman and I okay. Ruth Elder."

The captain reported that Elder seemed unfazed by the crash landing. "When she stepped to the deck of the ship, worn and wet and with her hair plastered to her head, she very politely thanked me and then reached into a bag for a mirror and lipstick to repair some of the damage that had been done to her makeup." His crew unsuccessfully attempted to salvage the airplane. As workers hoisted *American Girl* to the deck, the aircraft struck the ship's side. A wing crumpled and burst into flames. Crewmen quickly cut loose the airplane and dumped it into the ocean.

President Calvin Coolidge told reporters, "I am glad that they are safe." The pair had been lucky. If the SS *Barendrecht* had not been nearby, they would have perished in the cold Atlantic water. Although everyone who had followed their progress was relieved that the pair was safe, Elder and Haldeman immediately came under fire for what was now perceived as a very silly undertaking. Charles Lindbergh thought it had been a foolish gamble. The *Daily News* of London voiced the opinion that "their flight was an altogether unjustifiable risk in the present stage of air navigation. To try to fly the Atlantic in October is almost as suicidal as an attempt to shoot Niagara Falls in a barrel." Their financial backers weren't happy with Haldeman and Elder either. They had lost their $35,000 investment. Lyle Womack,

Elder's husband, also revealed his displeasure. When reached in Panama and asked if he would approve of another attempt by his wife, he stated, "Of course I would not."

Even women, who should have supported Ruth Elder, criticized her instead. Dr. Katherine B. Davis, a leader in the field of sociology, believed the flight was "a mistaken thing for a young girl to do. There is no woman alive today that I know of equipped for such a flight." Eleanor Roosevelt, always a supporter of women's rights, thought the effort by Haldeman and Elder was "very foolish." According to Winifred Sackville Stoner, a founder of the League for Fostering Genius, "A good typist is of much more service to humanity." Secretary of War Dwight F. Davis agreed with the women. He said, "Future transoceanic air flights are useless and a wanton gamble of lives and money unless they have some definite scientific purpose."

Fortunately, those in the world of aviation believed otherwise. Aviation legends Clarence Chamberlin, Guiseppe M. Bellanca, Grover Loening, Herman M. Fairchild, and Edgar N. Gott disagreed with the opinion that the flight had been a waste of time or money. Some believed that the pair should have chosen a different airplane or waited for better flying conditions. Nevertheless, they all felt that the flight had scientific value. Elder and Haldeman had pioneered a new transatlantic route, flown in the face of poor weather, and almost achieved their goal.

Several thousand people welcomed Elder and Haldeman when the SS *Barendrecht* reached the Azores. After several days of much-needed rest, Elder and Haldeman left for Lisbon, Portugal. Aboard the steamship *Lima*, Elder told reporters that she intended to try another transatlantic flight in August 1928. When the pair arrived in Lisbon, exactly fourteen days after their departure from Roosevelt Field, they were treated like conquering heroes and received a royal welcome.

Leaving Lisbon by air, Elder and Haldeman took turns with the Portuguese pilots at the controls of the military airplane. Meanwhile, back in Florida, movie, theater, and advertising companies besieged Thomas McArdle with offers to tell the Elder and Haldeman story. According to McArdle, one company had offered $50,000 for the pair to appear as Queen Guinevere and King Arthur while advertising indoor greyhound racing. Cold-cream, cigarette, and soft-drink companies all wanted Elder as a spokesperson.

Just as they had departed Roosevelt Field from virtually the same spot as Lindbergh had, Haldeman landed the airplane at the Paris airfield within a few feet of where Lindbergh had come to a stop five months earlier. Elder told the several thousand people gathered to greet them, "I'll do it yet. I am determined to show the world that what man can do, woman also can do." Elder and Haldeman left Cherbourg, France, aboard the British luxury liner *Aquatania* on November 5, arriving in New York six days later.

A representative of the National Women's Party was the first person to greet Elder in New York. A police escort led them to a welcoming reception by Mayor Jimmy Walker. Elder's husband, Lyle Womack, was lost in the shuffle. When newspapermen constantly referred to him as Mr. Elder, he was not amused. Ruth Elder was guest of honor at a dinner hosted by Mr. and Mrs. William Randolph Hearst. The mayor, royalty, society figures, and leaders of American industry also attended. Days later, the Advertising Club of New York honored her with the City of Paris Medal.

On November 13, Haldeman and Elder were guests of President Coolidge at a White House event celebrating the accomplishments of several men and women who had attempted to fly across the Atlantic Ocean. Included among the guests were Charles Lindbergh, Clarence D. Chamberlin, and Richard E. Byrd. The National Women's Party also entertained Elder and Haldeman at several functions.

The attempt by Ruth Elder and George Haldeman to fly across the Atlantic Ocean wasn't really a failure. Every flier who tried to cross the Atlantic made it easier for others to follow. Elder and Haldeman had established an over-water endurance flight record of 2,623 miles. Elder had been the pilot for at least nine of the flight's twenty-eight hours. Her achievement gave new hope to women fliers.

Capitalizing on her attempt to cross the Atlantic, Ruth Elder took part in a twenty-five-week lecture tour promoted by Loew's Vaudeville. The money was good. She received $5,000 each week to tell her story. She was the star of the show. Haldeman received similar offers for only one-tenth of the money Elder was paid. In June

1928, she signed a film contract, playing in silent movies with Hoot Gibson and Richard Dix. Just as quickly as she made money, she spent it and was soon broke. In 1929, she entered the first Women's Air Derby, but a fourth-place finish effectively ended her aviation career.

Married six times, Elder told her story in her own words when she wrote her autobiography. When asked why she had wanted to be the first woman to fly the Atlantic Ocean, she offered two answers. She just wanted to be the first, plus she had a "desire to buy an evening dress." She wanted a Paris dress and saw no reason why she shouldn't fly to Europe to buy it!

Amelia Mary Earhart is undoubtedly the world's best-known female flier. Born July 24, 1897, in Atchison, Kansas, she came from a well-to-do family. Her education included studies at Ogontz School, a college preparatory program in Philadelphia, and New York's Columbia University.

Earhart's interest in aviation developed when she visited her sister in Toronto, Canada, in 1917 and saw firsthand the effects of World War I. She was so moved by the sight of injured Royal Canadian Air Force pilots that she dropped out of school to work as a nurse's aide at Toronto's Spadina Military Hospital. In her spare time, she watched students from the Royal Flying Corps at a nearby field. One day when an airplane flew low above her, she wrote in her journal, "Mingled fear and pleasure winged over me. I believe that little red airplane said something to me as it swished by."

When she finally took her first airplane ride, she was immediately hooked. "As soon as we left the ground, I knew I myself had to fly." Earhart began taking flying lessons from Neta Snook, a female flight instructor. The twenty-four-year-old pilot received her license on December 15, 1921. Interest in aviation was at an all-time high. Records were being set, broken, and set again. After Charles Lindbergh made his solo flight across the Atlantic in 1927, people immediately began to clamor for a transatlantic crossing by a woman.

Following Charles Lindbergh's phenomenal accomplishment, Amy Phipp Guest, an American living in England, had offered to pay the expenses of a transatlantic flight by a woman. Well-known publisher George Palmer Putnam led the search for the right woman to make the ocean crossing. When he heard about Earhart, Putnam arranged a meeting in April 1928. With his flair for marketing, he recognized immediately that he had a winner in Earhart. Amelia even looked somewhat like Lindbergh. The public and the press loved it when Putnam began calling Amelia Earhart "Lady Lindy."

Earhart made her first transatlantic crossing on June 17, 1928, using a three-engine Fokker named *Friendship*. On the flight between Trepassey, Newfoundland, and Burry Port, Wales, Wilmer Stultz was pilot; Louis Gordon served as copilot and mechanic. Amelia Earhart was only a passenger on the flight, but she received all of the attention. The press made her an overnight celebrity. During the six months following the flight, she gave more than 200 interviews and 100 speeches. Earhart was a strong defender of jobs for women. She also actively worked toward the promotion of commercial aviation and the cause of peace.

In August 1929, Earhart flew in America's first aerial race for women, the Women's Air Derby. The cross-country event was part of the annual air races sponsored by the National Aeronautics Association. When a man derisively referred to the women's race as the Powder Puff Derby, the name stuck. Earhart finished third, but more importantly, she came up with the idea of an association for women pilots. Since there were ninety-nine original members, Earhart suggested calling the organization the Ninety-Nines. She immediately became the group's first president. At the same time, the relationship between Earhart and Putnam moved from professional to personal. They were married on February 7, 1931.

The following year, Amelia Earhart Putnam did what no other woman had ever done. She flew across the Atlantic Ocean alone. On May 20, 1932, in her single-engine Lockheed Vega, she left Harbor Grace, Newfoundland. Fifteen hours and eighteen minutes later, the fastest crossing of the Atlantic Ocean to date, she landed near Londonderry, Ireland. For her accomplishment she received the Cross of the French Legion of Honor, the Harmon Trophy for best woman pilot of the year, and the National Geographic Society's gold medal.

On July 29, 1932, she became the first woman to receive the Distinguished Flying Cross from the United States Congress.

Over the next several years, Earhart increased her reputation as the world's best-known woman pilot. In 1935 she became the first person, man or woman, to fly alone across the Pacific Ocean from Hawaii to San Francisco. That same year, she also set a record by flying across the Gulf of Mexico from Mexico City to Newark, New Jersey. At Purdue University in Indiana, she served as a career counselor for women and an advisor in aeronautics.

Publicity campaigns, her husband's money, her charm, and even a physical resemblance to Charles Lindbergh contributed to Amelia Earhart's fame. Her reputation may have been greater than her skill as a pilot. From the very beginning of her flying career, skeptics questioned her ability as an aviator. Nevertheless, Earhart had accomplished almost everything that any flier, male or female, could want. First she conquered the Atlantic, then the Pacific. No woman had ever made a flight around the world. Amelia Earhart wanted to be the first. Months of planning went into her round-the-world trip. First she chose her route around the equator, a distance of 29,000 miles. Then she picked an airplane. She chose a Lockheed Electra that Purdue University had purchased as a flying laboratory.

Earhart started her trip on March 17, 1937, flying west from Oakland, California, to the Hawaiian Islands. Leaving Hawaii, her airplane tipped over and suffered considerable damage. Extensive repairs grounded the aircraft for two months. Meanwhile, George Putnam and Amelia Earhart decided to try something different. She would reverse her route and fly east instead of west. That would put the most difficult part of the trip at the end.

Earhart left California on May 20 and arrived in Miami, Florida, three days later. At 5:56 A.M. on June 1, she and her copilot/navigator, Fred Noonan, departed Miami's municipal airport headed for San Juan, Puerto Rico. In an effort to reduce weight, Earhart decided to leave behind her trailing radio antenna. It was a bad decision.

From Puerto Rico, Earhart and Noonan crossed to the eastern coast of Central and South America. The pair then flew across the South Atlantic to Africa before going on to India and Southeast Asia. On the morning of July 2, they left Lae, New Guinea. In just thirty days, they had traveled 22,000 miles. The toughest part of the flight lay ahead of them. They still had to fly 2,556 miles across the Pacific before refueling at Howland Island.

As Earhart's aircraft neared Howland on the morning of July 2, the U.S. Coast Guard ship *Itasca* picked up a radio message. Earhart reported that her aircraft was running low on gas. An hour later, all signals stopped. No one ever heard from Amelia Earhart or Fred Noonan again.

A massive search, which spared no expense, took place. Nothing was found. Different theories tried to explain Earhart's disappearance. Some thought that she had been on a spy mission for the United States. Others believed the Japanese executed her after a crash landing. The most likely explanation was that her airplane ran out of gas, crashed into the ocean, and sank. Whatever the cause, the end result was the same. The best-known woman flier of all time was lost without a trace.

Despite the tragedy, Earhart furthered the cause of all women fliers. Regardless of her successes or failures, she helped the public to see flying as more than a technical achievement. She was an example of human courage and lofty dreams. In the minds of many people, Amelia Earhart symbolizes the best of women pilots.

WORLD WAR II

Chapter Four

World War II

Patriotic Americans tried to do their part in all kinds of ways during World War II. Flying for the military seemed like a logical way for pilots to serve their country. Unfortunately, not everyone agreed. The War Department and the aviation branch of the U.S. Army felt that the idea made sense only if the pilot was a white male. After an extended battle, the Army Air Forces admitted African-American men to flight training. For female aviators, regardless of their race, there were few choices.

Eleanor Roosevelt, wife of the president of the United States, strongly supported the efforts of women pilots. In her column in the *Washington Daily News,* she frequently stated that women should have an equal opportunity for noncombat service. The first lady believed skilled female pilots were important weapons for fighting the war. They were just waiting to be used.

Not everyone agreed. Most men, including high-ranking military and government officials, firmly opposed women joining the armed forces, especially as pilots. In 1941, the *Congressional Record* put it bluntly: "Take the women into the Armed Service, who then will do the cooking, the washing, the mending, the humble homey tasks to which every woman has devoted herself? Think of the humiliation! What has become of the manhood of America!"

Two women, Nancy Harkness Love and Jacqueline Cochran, saw things differently. They were determined to change the government's thinking. Commanded by Pauline Gower, women pilots in England had been flying as members of the Royal Air Force Air Transport Auxiliary (ATA) since 1940. The ATA pilots were playing an important role in the British war effort. Love and Cochran knew that women had valuable aviation skills that could help the American cause. They just needed to be given a chance.

Months before the United States entered the war, Jacqueline Cochran made history. She did something no other woman had ever done. Cochran copiloted a Lockheed Hudson bomber from an American factory, across the Atlantic Ocean, to a military base in England. That feat gave her the chance to meet with the commanding general of the Army Air Forces, Henry "Hap" Arnold, and Colonel Robert Olds, the officer in charge of the Ferry Command. Cochran immediately presented her plan for using the aviation skills of American women pilots.

General Arnold urged Cochran to go to England and study the British ATA program firsthand. Jacqueline Cochran and twenty-three other American women that she recruited began service with the Royal Air Force early in 1942. Several months later, Arnold ordered Cochran to return to America. He wanted her to organize and direct a new project. It would train women pilots for service with the Army Air Forces.

When she arrived home, Jacqueline Cochran learned that someone else had just been put in charge of a program for women pilots. Twenty-eight-year-old Nancy Harkness Love had been one of the women who took part in Phoebe Omlie's national air-marking program before the war. She was also a skilled pilot, with more than 1,200 flight hours to her credit. Now she would direct the Women's Auxiliary Ferrying Squadron (WAFS). Its members would ferry aircraft from the factories to military bases. That would free male pilots for combat duty.

Ten days later, on September 15, Jacqueline Cochran was named director of the 319th Army Air Forces Flying Detachment (Women). More commonly known as the Women's Flying Training Detachment (WFTD), it would operate at the same time as Nancy Love's program. Only months earlier, women pilots had no chance to fly in the war effort. Now, suddenly, they had two choices.

More than eighty female pilots were invited to apply for positions in the very exclusive Women's Auxiliary Ferrying Squadron. Twenty-eight actually served as WAFS pilots. Already licensed as commercial pilots, the group included some of the most qualified female fliers in America. All had at least 500 hours of flight time. Many had more than 1,000 hours in their logbooks. For example, Betty Huyler Gillies was one of the first women to report to New Castle Army Air Field on September 7, 1942. She was a former president of the Ninety-Nines. She owned her own airplane, a twin-engine amphibian. A licensed pilot since 1928, Gillies had worked for Grumman Aircraft.

The WAFS were sworn in as civilian pilots of the Air Transport Command. Then the female fliers received flight overalls, parachutes, goggles, and a silk Army Air Forces scarf. Each woman was paid $250 per month. Classes, which included navigation, ferry routes, military terms, and paperwork, lasted four weeks.

The first task for the WAFS pilots was to fly five single-engine Piper Cub airplanes from the factory at Lock Haven, Pennsylvania, to Mitchell Field, New York, on October 22, 1942. The ferry assignment went off without a hitch. By the end of the year, members of the WAFS were delivering all types of military aircraft to bases around the country. At first, the WAFS operated out of New Castle Army Air Force Base in Delaware. Soon Nancy Love's program had three more ferrying bases in Dallas, Texas; Long Beach, California; and Romulus, Michigan.

Meanwhile, news of the Women's Flying Training Detachment (WFTD), under Jacqueline Cochran's command, spread. Thousands of applications poured in. The main purpose of the program was to see if women could serve as military pilots. If they could, then the program would be the start of an organization that could be rapidly expanded to release male pilots for combat.

The WFTD was planned as a larger, more extensive program than that of the Women's Auxiliary Ferrying Squadron. WFTD training would be based at Howard Hughes Municipal Airport, next door to Ellington Army Air Field in Houston, Texas. Leni Leoti "Dedie" Deaton was a married thirty-nine-year-old mother of an eighteen-year-old son. Now she had a new job as chief staff executive officer. One of her primary duties would be to look after the young women in the program.

Cochran required that "her girls" be American citizens between twenty-one and thirty-five years of age. A minimum height requirement of five feet later increased to five feet, four inches. The minimum age eventually dropped to eighteen and one-half. Two hundred hours of logged flying experience later decreased to at least thirty-five hours. Applicants also had to pass a rigorous physical exam by a flight physician.

Class 43-W-1 of the Women's Flying Training Detachment began instruction on November 16, 1942. Aviation Enterprises, Limited, a civilian company, taught military flying. Military pilots provided qualifying check flights. More than 400 hours of ground school included classes in aircraft design, theory of flight, mathematics, physics, weather, code, and navigation. Before graduation, 210 hours of flight instruction had to be completed. At least eight hours of dual time with an instructor took place before the female trainees could solo.

The twenty-seven-week, flight-training program was dangerous and difficult. Twenty-eight women entered the first class. Only twenty-three graduated. Rates of elimination varied for later classes, but on average, the women did better than male flight cadets. As more women entered Cochran's program, flying conditions in Houston became more crowded and dangerous. Early in 1943, the Women's Flying Training Detachment operation moved to the larger, better-equipped Avenger Field, just outside of Sweetwater, Texas.

On August 5, 1943, Cochran's WFTD training program and the WAFS pilots, under Nancy Harkness Love's command, merged into the Women Airforce Service Pilots (WASP) program. Jacqueline Cochran was appointed as director. Love became staff director for all WASP members who were assigned as ferry pilots in the Air Transport Command division. Pilots in both the WAFS and the WFTD had been considered civil service employees. The WASP program was no different. Although they were flying military aircraft and performing other types of service-related duties, the female pilots were not members of the armed forces. Therefore, they received no military benefits.

Being a WASP trainee wasn't a glamorous experience. It was hard, dangerous work. Wind-burned skin replaced carefully applied make-up. Oversized, surplus, army mechanics' coveralls took the place of fashionable civilian clothing. Upon graduation, the trainees received their silver wings. They also wore their dress uniform of a matching Santiago-blue skirt and jacket with a white shirt. Accessories included a beret, a black tie, gloves, stockings, and black-leather dress shoes with a 2¼-inch heel. Flying attire wasn't as fancy. Dark-colored slacks, blue shirts, and laced-up shoes were more functional.

No one got rich flying as a member of the WASP. The women paid for their own transportation to Oklahoma. If they were eliminated from the program, they had to pay their own way back home. Trainees were paid $150 per month. Regulation overtime gave them an extra $22.50 each month. While training at Sweetwater, each woman paid the government $1.65 per day for room and board.

After assignment to operational duties, each flier received a monthly base pay of $250, plus an additional $37.50 in overtime. From that amount, she paid $15-$20 per month for her living quarters. Six dollars per day covered the pilot's expenses while away from base. If a female flier crashed and died in the line of duty, there was no flag-draped coffin, no military funeral. Her fellow pilots had to take up a collection to cover the cost of returning her body to her family.

Most male flight cadets learned to fly on one or two types of aircraft before moving into a single kind of aircraft. Not so with the women. After graduation from the training program, the female pilots ferried nearly every type of aircraft in the fleet of the United States Army Air Forces. They flew PT-17s, PT-19s, BT-13s, BT-15s, AT-6s, AT-17s, P-40s, P-47s, P-51s, B-17s, B-26s, B-29s, C-54s, and more. The women towed targets while fighter aircraft practiced shooting at them. They also flew recently repaired aircraft to make sure the planes were airworthy. One WASP even tested the Army Air Forces' new jet plane.

By January 1, 1944, more than 1,000 women were either in training or on active duty as Women Airforce Service Pilots. On the surface, things seemed to be going well. In fact, it was the beginning of the end for the program. On February 17, 1944, California representative John Costello proposed a bill to the House Committee on Military Affairs.

The legislation would make the WASPs members of the military rather than of the civil service.

Savage and unrelenting protest against Costello's bill was quick in coming. With male fliers out of work, the press wanted to know why the government would train women to take men's jobs. The American Legion actively argued against the WASP program. A campaign of misinformation circulated rumors about the relationship between General Henry Arnold and Jacqueline Cochran.

An article in *Time* magazine classified the Women Airforce Service Pilots as an expensive experiment that was both unnecessary and undesirable. On June 5, 1944, the Civil Service Committee concluded that the WASP program was a waste of time and effort. Newspaperman Drew Pearson wrote an especially nasty column against Jacqueline Cochran in the *Washington Times-Herald* on June 14. One week later, the bill to militarize the Women Airforce Service Pilots, H.R. 4219, was defeated by only nineteen votes.

On June 26, 1944, General Henry Arnold announced the end of the WASP program. Women already at Avenger Field would be allowed to complete their flight training. The forty-eight members of class 45-W-1, who had recently arrived at the Texas airfield, were sent home. By August, 125 female pilots had been released. On October 3, the women remaining on active duty in the WASP program received two letters. The one from Jacqueline Cochran told them what a great job they had done. The second letter came from General Arnold. It stated that the WASP program would be deactivated on December 20, 1944.

The last WASP class, 44-W-10, graduated on December 7, 1944. At the graduation ceremonies at Avenger Field, General Barton Yount and Commanding General of the Army Air Forces Henry Arnold both addressed the sixty-eight women. Yount praised their courage and talked about how important the WASP program had been to the war effort. Arnold said, "The WASP have completed their mission. Their job has been successful. But as is usual in war, the cost has been heavy. Thirty-eight WASP have died while helping their country move toward the moment of final victory. The Air Forces will long remember their service and their final sacrifice." Class 44-W-10 had graduated, but there was nothing to celebrate.

They had nowhere to report for duty, no jobs to do, no airplanes to fly. They were sent home.

Of the more than 25,000 women who applied, 1,830 had been accepted into the program; 1,074 earned their wings. By December 1944, there were still 916 women on duty—141 with the Air Transport Command, 620 with the Training Command, and another 155 assigned to the domestic air forces and weather wings. The WASP pilots had flown more than sixty million miles, averaging thirty-three hours of flying time each month. They had flown seventy-seven different types of aircraft during 12,650 missions. Thirty-eight had died while serving a country that did not want them to fly.

The eloquent words of Generals Arnold and Yount were meaningless. There was no GI bill of rights, no life insurance, no medical coverage, no educational assistance, and no financial help with home mortgages. The women were discharged from service with only the satisfaction that they had served their country and accomplished something that many said couldn't be done.

Recognition for the women who took part in the organizations commanded by Jacqueline Cochran and Nancy Harkness Love was slow to arrive. Finally, on November 23, 1977, President Jimmy Carter signed into law WASP legislation providing military benefits for the women. In 1984, each woman pilot received a long overdue Victory Medal. Those who had been on duty for at least one year received the American Theater Medal.

GREAT STRIDES

Chapter Five

Great Strides

The first flight of the Wright brothers took place in 1903. Since then, women have made great strides in the field of aviation. Unfortunately, aviation's still pretty much a man's world. While there has been progress, there's still a long way to go. Women make up over fifty percent of the population, yet less than fifteen percent of the approximately 80,000 airline pilots are women.

Helen Richey, of McKeesport, Pennsylvania, made history as the first female airline pilot in the United States. After graduation from high school, she decided to take flying lessons. She made her first solo flight in 1930. She then began building up her flying experience, setting aviation records, and winning several air races.

On December 20, 1933, Helen Richey and Frances Harrell Marsalis took off from Miami's municipal airport. They intended to set a new record for spending the most hours in the air without landing. Newspaper reporters nicknamed their airplane the *Flying Boudoir*. The pilots carried only a small amount of gasoline with them. Another airplane, flown by Jack Loesing and Fred Fetterman, would refuel their aircraft in midair.

Throughout their flight, the women experienced some of the worst weather conditions that south Florida could offer. They flew through dense fog, heavy rainstorms, threatening lightning, and intense heat. As if that wasn't enough, during one attempted refueling, the heavy gas cans ripped open the cloth-covered wing of their airplane. Marsalis continued to fly the plane. Richey climbed out onto the wing to make repairs before the fabric ripped away.

On December 28, they surpassed the old record of eight days, four hours, and five minutes in the air. They were exhausted, but they weren't ready to land yet. Two days later, they were still in the air, even though they could barely stay awake. Originally, they took turns piloting in two-hour shifts. Now the women switched to one hour at the controls and one hour off, since they were so tired. Making it worse yet, heavy rains and high winds battered their small airplane as they flew.

On the morning of December 30, they finally landed their oil-and-gasoline-soaked aircraft. Helen Richey and Frances Marsalis had set a new endurance record. They had kept their airplane in the air without landing for nine days, twenty-one hours, and forty-two minutes.

The following year, Helen Richey sought out Dick Coulter, owner of Central Airlines. She wanted a new challenge. She wanted a job as an airline pilot. As she competed with several men for the job, she heard all of the arguments against her. They said she was too small, too weak, and too inexperienced. If that weren't enough, they argued that she would be taking a job away from a man. To her surprise, Dick Coulter hired her anyway.

On December 31, 1934, Richey made her first flight for Central Airlines. She piloted a Ford Trimotor from Washington, DC, to Detroit, Michigan. It wasn't going to be a regular event, however. Richey wasn't allowed to fly in bad weather. In fact, she seldom had a chance to fly at all. She wasn't permitted to join the pilots' union. Her male counterparts made it obvious that they resented her and didn't want her flying with them. It seemed that Dick Coulter had only hired her as a publicity gimmick to win passengers in the competition between Central Airlines and Pennsylvania Airlines.

Helen Richey's career with Central Airlines came to an early end when she resigned in October 1935. During her ten months with the airline, she had probably flown no more than a dozen round trips. Nevertheless, she had broken down one more barrier.

Her flying career did not end with her disappointing experience at Central Airlines, however. Richey joined Phoebe Omlie's air-marking program along with other well-known women pilots such as Louise von Thaden, Blanche Noyes, and Nancy Harkness Love. She continued to take part in exhibitions and races. In 1936, Richey teamed up with Amelia Earhart for the cross-country Bendix Trophy Race. They came in fifth.

Like many Americans, Helen Richey wanted to help England in its fight against Germany during World War II. She applied to the British Air Transport Auxiliary for a pilot's position. When she arrived in England in 1942, Richey was certainly well qualified. She was a member of the Ninety-Nines. She had nearly 2,000 hours of flying experience, a commercial license, and her instructor's rating. She had also served as a flight instructor for the United States Army Air Corps. Unfortunately, attitudes toward women fliers were no different in England. The arguments were the same. Flying was not a suitable profession for women. They were taking jobs from men. Nevertheless, Richey was one of almost thirty American women to fly with Britain's Air Transport Auxiliary.

In January 1943, Richey returned to the United States. She soon found herself in the Women Airforce Service Pilots program. A member of the fifth class to graduate, she completed training at Avenger Field on September 11, 1943. For the next several months, Richey ferried twin-engine Mitchell B-25 bombers throughout the United States. When the WASP program ended in 1944, America's first woman airline pilot was once again out of work. In January 1947, Helen Richey committed suicide at the age of only thirty-seven.

Although Central Airlines hired Helen Richey as a pilot back in 1934, progress would be slow after that. A major American airline wouldn't hire a female pilot for nearly forty more years. Back in 1958, when she was just seventeen, Emily Howell Warner had flown for the first time as a passenger aboard a Frontier Airlines DC-3. She enjoyed it so much that she signed up for flying lessons. At first she dreamed of becoming a flight attendant but was soon convinced that she could become a pilot. A job as a receptionist at a flight school based at Denver's Stapleton International Airport gave her the chance. She flew as often as possible, building flying experience.

In 1967, nine years after her first airplane ride, Warner began apply-
ing for jobs as a pilot with the airlines. It was a task that would take
several years. Finally, on January 29, 1973, Frontier Airlines hired her
as a second officer. The door was inching open. Two months later,
American Airlines hired Bonnie Tiburzi.

On February 6, 1973, Emily Howell Warner made her first flight for
Frontier, a trip from Denver to Las Vegas. Her male counterparts
weren't quick to accept her into their ranks. In fact, they certainly didn't
do anything to make it easy. Supposedly, on her second flight, the captain advised her not to touch anything on the airplane. That seemed
like a good indication of his lack of faith in her skills!

Warner persevered and was promoted to first officer the following year. By 1976 she was flying as captain. With each accomplishment, she broke another barrier. She was the first woman to
fly as a second officer, first officer, and, eventually, captain for a
major American airline. She was the first female member of the
Airline Pilots Association. On July 5, 1984, Emily Howell Warner
again made history. She flew as captain, and Linda Christopherson
served as first officer aboard a Boeing 737 flight. They were part
of the first all-female flight crew.

Captain Warner flew not only for Frontier Airlines, but also for
Continental Airlines and United Parcel Service. After a career filled
with impressive awards, and with thousands of flight hours on her
résumé, Emily Howell Warner retired in 2002 at the age of sixty-two.
Her philosophy had been simple. She believed that the airplane didn't
know if the pilot was male or female. The pilot just needed to get the
job done.

Jacqueline Cochran was one of America's top aviators. Much of her
early life is a mystery. Jacqueline Cochran was not her real name.
Foster parents may have given her the name, or, perhaps, she chose the
name herself from a telephone book because she liked the way it
sounded. Sometime between 1905 and 1912 is as close as anyone can
get regarding her birth date. No one knows for sure where she was
born, but it was probably somewhere near Pensacola, Florida.

What is certain is that Jacqueline Cochran was one of the twentieth century's most celebrated pilots—female or male. Her flying career was a list of firsts. She did things that no one believed a woman could do. She led the way for American women to serve as pilots in the British Air Transport Auxiliary as well as in the Women Airforce Service Pilots program during World War II. Her accomplishments in the cockpit of an airplane were legendary.

Jacqueline Cochran overcame a less-than-ideal childhood. She refused to let a lack of money hold her back and was determined to escape a life filled with poverty. As a young girl with a very limited formal education, Cochran worked at beauty parlors in Florida and Alabama. In 1929, she moved to New York City, where she worked as a beautician. Then she started her own cosmetics company.

Cochran met and, in 1932, married Floyd Odlum, a wealthy financier. It was his idea for her to learn to fly. Odlum believed that it would give her a competitive edge in the cosmetics business. Cochran made arrangements for lessons at Roosevelt Flying School at Long Island, New York. Some accounts claim that she received her pilot's license after only three weeks' training. Others reported that it actually took six weeks.

In either case, Cochran loved flying and was very good at it. But even two months' worth of flying lessons weren't enough to make a good pilot, and she knew it. In 1933, Jacqueline Cochran enrolled in the Ryan School of Flying in San Diego for further instruction. She earned her commercial license and bought her first airplane, a used TravelAir.

It didn't take Cochran long to make newspaper headlines. She announced that she was going to take part in the MacRobertson London-Melbourne Race. The contest would celebrate the 100th anniversary of the founding of Victoria, Australia. The nearly 12,000-mile race included some of the world's best-known aviators. Cochran would someday be a member of that elite group, but she wasn't there yet. It was a bold undertaking for someone who had been flying for only two years.

Sixty-four airplanes registered for the event. Along with Cochran and her copilot, Wesley Smith, there were two other American teams.

By the day of the race, there were only twenty participants still in the contest. Most had dropped out. On the rainy morning of October 20, 1934, nearly 60,000 people waited at Mildenhall, England, for the race to begin. Even the king and queen of England, as well as the Prince of Wales, were there. At 6:30 A.M., the white flag dropped, signaling the start of the event. Jacqueline Cochran and Wesley Smith were the fourth team in the air. While heading down the runway, their Granville Q.E.D. airplane hit a ridge and threatened to crash. Somehow they managed to take off, but it wasn't a good beginning.

Cochran's first major air race had been plagued by difficulties even before the competition began. Neither pilot had much experience with the airplane. Smith had about two hours' flying time on the aircraft. Cochran had even less. Two days before the race, they had problems with the airplane's flaps. Once in the air, the only woman in the race didn't fare any better. Mechanical problems with their airplane forced them to land in Bucharest, Rumania. The race was over for Cochran and Smith.

The Bendix Trophy Race, sponsored by the Bendix Aviation Corporation, was one of the most important aviation events in the United States in the 1930s. Unfortunately, the transcontinental race was for men only. When it opened to women in 1933, Amelia Earhart entered and finished fifth. In 1935, both Jacqueline Cochran and Amelia Earhart were contestants. Earhart again came in fifth. Cochran's plane had engine problems and didn't finish the race. Two years later, Cochran finished in third place, winning a $2,000 prize.

Each year, the open-course, coast-to-coast race drew some of the best-known aviators in America. In 1938, Jacqueline Cochran was the only woman entered in the competition. Cochran made the 2,000-mile trip from Los Angeles to Cleveland in slightly over eight hours. Her Seversky AP-7 had an average speed of almost 250 miles per hour. At 2:23 P.M. on September 23, Cochran crossed the finish line to win the Bendix Trophy Race and its $12,500 prize. She also received the Harmon Trophy, naming her as the outstanding female pilot of the previous year.

Jacqueline Cochran was well known for her feistiness, for doing things her own way, and for making things happen. She was also famous for setting a host of aviation records. On March 24, 1939, high above Palm Springs, California, Cochran established a woman's altitude flying record of 30,052 feet. In September she broke the international open-class speed record for men and women. She also found time, in a very busy schedule, to win the New York-Miami Air Race. The following year, she set two new speed records.

World War II deeply affected Jacqueline Cochran. She devoted all of her efforts to helping the Allies achieve victory. For some American women, doing your part for the war meant growing victory gardens or volunteering for the Red Cross. For others it meant working in factories and shipyards. For Jacqueline Cochran, it first meant flying with the British Air Transport Auxiliary in England. Months after that, it meant serving as head of the Women Airforce Service Pilots program in America.

With the end of the war, the world of aviation began to return to normal. Jacqueline Cochran was back in the cockpit, setting aviation records. She purchased a P-51 Mustang and entered the Bendix Trophy Race in 1946. She came in second. Flying the same P-51 in 1950, Cochran set an international speed record for propeller-driven airplanes. That year, the Harmon Trophy committee named her as the outstanding female pilot of the 1940s.

Like many pilots of the propeller-driven-aircraft era, Jacqueline Cochran wanted to move up a step. She wanted to fly as fast as possible. She wanted to fly jets! She also wanted to be the first woman pilot to break the sound barrier. That presented several real problems. She needed an airplane that could fly fast enough, a place to fly it, and someone to teach her. Edwards Air Force Base in California was the most logical place, but it was a military installation. Jacqueline Cochran, however, was not one to let problems stop her from getting what she wanted.

Somehow, she convinced the United States Air Force to allow her to train at Edwards. Then she persuaded Air Force pilot Charles "Chuck" Yeager, the first man to break the sound barrier, to teach her. All she still needed was an airplane. Getting her hands on a North American Aviation F-86 Sabre took care of that. On May 18, 1953, after months of training, it happened. Jacqueline Cochran did what no other woman had ever done. Flying the jet at more than 652 miles per hour, she broke the sound barrier.

In 1955, Jacqueline Cochran's life took on a new direction when she decided to run for political office. Winning a California House of Representatives seat seemed like a sure thing. Few people had greater name recognition than Jacqueline Cochran. This victory wasn't to be hers. In spite of her political connections and fame, she lost the election. There were other triumphs, however. The Fédération Aéronautique Internationale elected Cochran as its first woman president in 1958. Two years later, she was reelected.

In 1961, she again enlisted the help of her friend Chuck Yeager. This time she wanted him to teach her to fly the twin-engine Northrop T-38. Official hurdles needed to be overcome. If she was going to set new speed and altitude records, she needed a T-38. Unfortunately, the only T-38s available belonged to the United States Air Force, and they weren't about to loan one to a civilian. A little creativity was in order. Cochran once again made things happen.

The Air Force leased one of its T-38s back to Northrop Aircraft Corporation. The company then hired Cochran as a pilot and allowed her to use its leased T-38. As he had done in 1953, Chuck Yeager worked with Cochran for several weeks. Before 1961 ended, Cochran owned two new records. Flying the T-38 jet at a speed of 842.6 miles per hour, she claimed the world speed record for women. Cochran also set the altitude record for women by flying to an altitude of 56,071 feet. That's more than ten and one-half miles above the earth!

The following year was equally busy for Cochran, as she set more speed, distance, and altitude records. In 1962 she also became the first woman to fly a jet across the Atlantic Ocean. To achieve that distinction, she piloted a four-engine business jet named *Scarlett O'Hara* from Houston, Texas, to Hanover, England.

In 1963, Cochran became a consultant for the National Aeronautics and Space Administration. She was also working for Lockheed Aircraft Corporation. She continued to set both speed and distance records for the next few years, but her illustrious flying career was slowly coming to an end. Both Cochran and her husband, Floyd Odlum, were in poor health. After she sold her cosmetics company, the two began spending much of their time at their California ranch. Odlum died in 1976. Jacqueline Cochran, one of the world's most successful and best-known female aviators, died on August 9, 1980. Certainly no other woman, and only a very few men, had done more during the twentieth century to further the cause of aviation.

Betty Skelton got an early start on her aviation career. She was born on June 28, 1926, in Pensacola, Florida. When she was only twelve years old, her father, a flight instructor and airport operator, began teaching her to fly. When they turn sixteen, many young Americans get their drivers' licenses. At sixteen, Betty already had hundreds of flight hours in her logbook. By the end of high school, she had earned not only her private pilot's license, but also her commercial pilot's certificate and flight instructor's rating.

At the age of nineteen, Betty Skelton took up aerobatic flying with a vengeance. The well-known Clem Whittenbeck was her instructor. Her aerobatic feats included outside loops, outside snap rolls, and upside-down flying only ten feet above the ground. Skelton was a great believer in showmanship and audience participation. She performed one trademark trick during her shows that required two poles with a ribbon suspended between them. Two volunteers from the audience held the poles. Skelton would then fly her aircraft upside down in an attempt to pick up the ribbon. When they realized that the nose of her airplane was coming straight toward them, the frightened volunteers would drop the poles and run for safety. As Skelton maneuvered her plane around for a second pass, members of her act would grab up the poles. Flying upside down as her airplane roared toward the ribbon, Skelton would then snatch it skyward.

With red hair and brown eyes, she stood only five feet, three inches tall and weighed barely one hundred pounds. Nevertheless, Betty Skelton did much more than aerobatic tricks in an airplane. As she toured the United States with her plane, named *Little Stinker,* she won races and broke several aerial records. Just in 1948 alone, she won the All-American Air Maneuvers competition as well as the women's International Aerobatics championship.

On July 11, 1949, Skelton attempted to break the women's speed record of 412 miles per hour, held by Jacqueline Cochran. In a practice run over the closed three-kilometer course at Tampa, Florida, Skelton flew a converted North American P-51 Mustang. She hit a top speed of 421.9 miles per hour. Unfortunately for her quest, disaster struck. The borrowed airplane's engine exploded, preventing her from making an official run. Instead, she was forced to make a nonpowered dead-stick landing at nearby MacDill Air Force Base. Nonetheless, she had set an unofficial world's speed record for piston-engine aircraft.

Betty Skelton gave up flying in the early 1950s and turned her attention to another dangerous occupation controlled by men. She became a racecar driver. Just as she had with flying, she excelled. In the minds of many, however, she will always be remembered for her skills as an aerobatic flier. In recognition of her achievements, the National Air and Space Museum recently restored her airplane, *Little Stinker,* as part of its aircraft collection.

While Betty Skelton was a dominant force in women's aerobatic flying in the 1940s, Patty Wagstaff is one of the best-known female aerobatic pilots in the world today. Her father piloted 747s for Japan Airlines, and her sister flew 727s for Continental Airlines in Guam. Flying wasn't always part of Patty Wagstaff's life, however. She had a varied career. She worked as a model, waitress, diver, office manager, and even a television actor in Japan.

Patty Wagstaff's husband taught her to fly, but routine flying wasn't enough. Wagstaff went on to become the first woman to win the United States National Aerobatic Championship after the men's and women's competitions were combined. A member of the United States National Aerobatic team, she has been the U.S. National Aerobatic champion several times.

In 1994, Patty Wagstaff received the National Air and Space Museum Trophy for "extraordinary service to air and space technology." She has also won the Betty Skelton "First Lady of Aerobatics" Trophy on many occasions. Today Patty Wagstaff is not only a world-famous aerobatic champion. She is also an author, a flight instructor, and has even worked as a Hollywood stunt pilot.

Early on the morning of December 14, 1986, a strange-looking contraption lumbered down a runway at Edwards Air Force Base in California. Its long wings flapped like those of a giant bird, and it seemed to take forever to pick up speed. Finally, after struggling for a distance of 14,000 feet, *Voyager* took to the air and headed out over the Pacific Ocean.

The revolutionary airplane was made out of graphite, paper, and resin. It carried two daring pioneers. Jeana Yeager and Dick Rutan were about to embark on something that had never been done before. They were trying to make an around-the-world flight without landing or refueling even once. It would be a distance of almost 25,000 miles. If successful, they would be hailed as heroes. If they failed, they could possibly end up like Amelia Earhart. They could be lost forever.

Empty, *Voyager* weighed less than 2,000 pounds. After the aircraft was loaded with fuel, supplies, and crew, its weight ballooned to more than 11,000 pounds. The inside of the airplane was incredibly small. There was only a small, cramped off-duty space for the person not at the aircraft's controls.

The flight did not go as smoothly as Yeager and Rutan had hoped. They flew an average speed of 115 miles per hour at altitudes ranging between 8,000 and 15,000 feet. Unfortunately, they were faced with weather conditions they had hoped to avoid. Horrific storms, worries about running out of gas, and even engine failure were constant threats throughout the continuous nine-day flight.

Finally, on the morning of December 23, *Voyager* headed for a landing at Edwards Air Force Base. While Dick Rutan circled the field, Jeana Yeager turned a crank to lower the landing gear. Twenty-five thousand people turned out to greet the exhausted pair. Millions more were glued to their television sets. It was the successful end to what many called one of the most significant aviation events in the twentieth century.

During the flight, Yeager and Rutan set several aviation records. For their courage and foresight, they received numerous awards, including the Presidential Citizen's Medal. At the presentation ceremony, President Ronald Reagan said, "When we saw you coming home—so ungainly, yet so graceful—well, that's just about the best present America could have had." Once again, another barrier had been broken and a woman had been part of it.

GI JANE

Chapter Six

GI Jane

American women who wished to fly during World War II faced major difficulties. After the war, women who wanted to be military pilots met obstacles that were just as huge. It took a long, hard struggle before women could climb into the cockpits of fighter aircraft to defend this country.

On July 26, 1948, President Harry Truman issued Executive Order 9981. It stated, "There shall be equality of treatment and opportunity for all persons in the armed services without regard to race, color, religion or national origin." The order was a step up for African-Americans, but it really had little effect on women in the military. Just weeks earlier, however, President Truman had signed Public Law 625. The Women's Armed Services Integration Act of 1948 would make a difference.

All women in the armed forces had been classified as reservists, rather than as part of the regular military. Public Law 625 now offered women a future in the armed forces, but it would be very limited. There were plenty of restrictions. Only two percent of the total enlisted military population could be women. No more than ten percent of the enlisted women could be officers. Women would not be allowed to hold any rank above that of colonel. Women couldn't command male personnel. But the limitations didn't stop there.

Women in the military would not be allowed to serve in combat. That meant that women in the Air Force could not be assigned to aircraft that took part in wartime missions. Female members of the navy couldn't serve on ships or planes in battle situations. The law would permit women to serve in the military. At the same time, it made sure that they could hold only certain jobs, with little room for advancement.

For the next twenty years, nothing changed. Women joined the military, but their numbers and the jobs they were allowed to perform were limited. Breakthroughs were small—tiny first steps on a long road. For example, in 1966, Ensign Gale Anne Gordon of the United States Navy Reserve made history. She attended and even graduated from a class in aviation experimental psychology at the Naval Aerospace Medical Institute.

Finally in 1967 Congress eliminated the two percent quota on women in the enlisted ranks. Restrictions on the highest ranks that women could reach were also lifted. As he signed the changes, President Lyndon B. Johnson said, "There is no reason why we should not someday have a female chief of staff or even a female commander in chief."

Things were definitely beginning to change. In October 1972, Secretary of the Navy John Warner announced that women would be allowed to take part in flight training. The following year, Barbara Allen Rainey, Judith Neuffer, Rosemary Conaster Mariner, Jane Skiles O'Dea, Anna Scott Fuquoa, and Jo Ellen Drag Oslund entered the U.S. Navy's pilot-training program. Eleven months later, the six women earned the right to wear gold wings as the navy's first female aviators.

In a ceremony at Corpus Christi, Texas, on February 22, 1974, Lieutenant Junior Grade Barbara Rainey made history twice. She graduated as America's first female naval aviator. She was also the first woman pilot in any branch of the United States military. The women in the WASP program had flown for the military during World War II, but they had been classified as civilians.

A year later, Barbara Rainey became the first woman to qualify as a navy jet pilot. Unfortunately, she would also become the first female navy pilot to die in a crash. Rainey was serving as a flight instructor at Middleton Field Naval Base in Alabama. When her flight student crashed their airplane while practicing landings, Barbara Rainey died.

Then the U.S. Army began to train women as helicopter pilots. On June 4, 1974, Sally Murphy entered the history books as the army's first female aviator. It hadn't been easy for her. Originally, there were supposed to have been three women in training. Instead, she was the only woman in a class of twenty-four flight students. Most of the men made it quite clear that they didn't want her in the program. Almost every day Murphy faced sexism and resistance.

In 1976, the United States Air Force jumped on the bandwagon of those favoring women in military aviation. Air Force generals decided to include twenty women in two undergraduate pilot-training classes. Television, radio, and newspapers competed to cover the training program and interview the women involved. Enormous hoopla surrounded the experiment. All of the old arguments were trotted out, just as in the earliest days when women wanted to learn to fly. The program's opponents argued that females were too small, too slow, and too weak. Some even complained about their hair length.

Competition for the first class was fierce. Fifty-seven women applied for the precious twenty training slots. Connie Engel, Mary Donahue, Kathy LaSauce, Susan Rogers, Christine Schott, Sandra Scott, Victoria Crawford, Mary Livingston, Carol Scherer, and Kathleen Rambo were the first ten to be chosen. They entered Air Force pilot training on August 22, 1976. All of the women successfully graduated at Williams Air Force Base in Arizona, on September 2, 1977. Of the second class of ten women, six graduated.

Several things gave women the chance for careers in military aviation. The all-volunteer military was established in 1973. That made it harder to justify a limited role for more than half of the American population. The opening of the U.S. military academies to women in 1976 offered new opportunities. At the same time, the women's movement called for new and expanded roles for working women in general.

Women in the military were well on their way to breaking down a barrier that had existed since the armed forces began using airplanes. The U.S. Army, Navy, and Air Force all had women pilots, but they were still restricted to nonfighting roles. There was, however, strong argument for the idea that women pilots deserved to become combat pilots. It would take almost fifteen more years before that would happen.

Congress passed Public Law 102-190 in December 1991. It finally removed the regulation against women serving on combat ships and aircraft. However, that wasn't the complete story. The Department of Defense still had a rule barring women from assignments with a high risk of enemy fire. Women could become pilots, but they still couldn't be placed in situations where they might face the enemy.

Secretary of Defense Les Aspin took care of that problem. He ended the ban on April 28, 1993. Aspin directed, "Two years ago, Congress repealed the law that prohibited women from being assigned to combat aircraft. It is now time to implement that mandate and address the remaining restriction on the assignment of women." One more barrier had been overcome. Women could now serve on combat aircraft in combat situations.

The timing could not have been more perfect for Jean Marie Flynn. She was the first woman in the United States Air Force allowed to become a combat fighter-pilot. Second Lieutenant Flynn had already applied and been turned down for fighter-pilot flight training once. Finally, in April 1993, she was accepted into the program. At Luke Air Force Base in Arizona, she underwent six months of training on the F-15E Strike Eagle. On February 10, 1994, Jean Flynn graduated from the combat-training program. Other women would soon follow in her footsteps.

In 1994, the United States Navy introduced women into combat fighter squadrons. Shannon Lee Workman had graduated in 1988 from the United States Naval Academy. She qualified in a T-2 aircraft on the USS *Lexington* in December 1989 and in an A-4 Skyhawk the following May. Based at Naval Air Station Whidbey Island, Washington, in 1994, Workman made a total of sixteen carrier landings. Then, while the USS *Eisenhower* trained off the coast of Virginia, Workman made an additional twelve daytime and four nighttime carrier landings flying an EA-6B Prowler. The *Navy News Service* announced her accomplishment: "First Female Combat Pilot Passes Carrier Qualifications in February 1994 on USS *Eisenhower.*"

Next, the navy announced that female aviators would deploy with a battle group for the first time. Shannon Workman was to be one of four female aviators aboard the USS *Eisenhower.* With her would be Lieutenant Sally Fountain, Lieutenant Terry Bradford, and Lieutenant Commander Janet Marnane.

Introducing women to combat ships was bound to create some problems, but the navy seemed to want to make it work. Captain Mark Gemmill of the USS *Eisenhower* summed it up. He said that it made no more sense to prohibit women from ships than it did to bar men because of their hair color. Some things never change, however. Sally Fountain recalled one occasion when she called the carrier repair office and identified herself to a male sailor. He then hollered out to his boss that there was a lieutenant chick on the phone for him. Not an officer, not even a female officer, but a lieutenant chick!

Shannon Workman also ran into some problems. In January 1995, the press reported that she had to leave the USS *Eisenhower* because she had trouble with aircraft-carrier landings. Of course, this once again raised the old argument that women were not as qualified to fly as men were. It didn't matter that every year many men experienced the same problems as Shannon Workman without making newspaper headlines. It didn't matter that her superior officers had praised her as being incredibly talented.

The United States Marine Corps admitted women on August 12, 1918, in order to "Free a Marine to fight." Of course, those women performed only clerical jobs. Almost eighty years would pass before the Marine Corps would allow women to join the elite ranks of marine aviators. Sarah M. Deal was a graduate of Kent State University's acrospace flight technology program. She was commissioned as a marine second lieutenant in May 1992, but she had no hope of pilot training. She attended air-traffic-control school instead.

When the marines finally decided to open aviation training to women, Sarah Deal was the first female to attend flight school in Pensacola, Florida. Graduation ceremonies were held on April 21, 1995. Sarah Deal's father, a former marine himself, pinned his daughter's gold wings on her uniform. After Sarah Deal was promoted to captain in 1996, she was assigned to the Marine Air Station in San Diego, California. Her duties included piloting the Sikorsky CH-53E Super Stallion helicopter, used to transport supplies.

Lieutenant Kara Hultgreen awakened at 7 A.M. on October 25, 1994, at California's Naval Air Station Miramar. That afternoon, she was scheduled to make an aircraft-carrier qualification refresher flight.

Kara Hultgreen could easily have been the poster child for the new U.S. Navy—a navy that not only allowed women, but also encouraged them to do it all. Restrictions had been lifted. The sky was now the limit. Hultgreen seemed to have everything going for her. She had graduated from the University of Texas at Austin with a degree in aerospace engineering. She was bright, energetic, and extremely photogenic and loved to fly. These were all ideal assets for the navy's plan to fully integrate women as combat pilots.

Kara Hultgreen had been the only woman in her class at the Naval Aviation Candidate School in Pensacola, Florida. Following graduation in August 1989, she was assigned to Naval Air Station Key West, Florida. There she logged several hundred hours in the navy's A-6 Intruder. By the time of her scheduled refresher flight, she had more than 1,200 flight hours, including 218 in the F-14A Tomcat. Months earlier, Hultgreen had also completed the carrier-qualification phase of her aviation training with a total of fifty-eight aircraft-carrier landings. She loved flying and described her career as the greatest job in the entire world.

On the afternoon of October 25, 1994, Hultgreen sat in the front seat of the twin-engine F-14. Her radar intercept operator sat in the back of the $38-million airplane. Then the F-14 roared down the runway at Naval Air Station Miramar. Within seconds, the jet was in the air, headed out over the Pacific Ocean. Weather and visibility were good as Hultgreen flew around for almost an hour. In the water below, the aircraft carrier USS *Abraham Lincoln* steamed along at about fifteen knots. It had been almost two months since Hultgreen's last carrier landing.

Just before 3 P.M., she began her approach to the carrier. Everything seemed normal. Then an incredibly fast sequence of events took place. The carrier's landing signal officer advised Hultgreen that she was coming in too fast. Her plane was waved off. Seconds later, black smoke trailed from the F-14's right engine. Hultgreen was ordered to level her wings and climb. Suddenly, the F-14 Tomcat rolled. Her radar intercept officer ejected from the out-of-control airplane and was rescued less than five minutes later. Kara Hultgreen stayed with the jet as it smashed into the Pacific Ocean. According to an official navy report, her body was still belted to the jet's ejection seat when it was recovered nineteen days later. Hultgreen's military funeral was held at Arlington National Cemetery.

Her death immediately set off a new firestorm regarding women pilots in the military. Critics argued that she had been incapable of handling the sophisticated F-14 aircraft. Many claimed that Hultgreen and other women in the military programs were given unfair advantages over their male counterparts. Others alleged that naval aviation-training standards had been lowered in order to have more female aviators than the Air Force had. Things would only get worse. The navy originally believed that engine failure caused the crash. A later report seemed to blame pilot error due to special treatment resulting from a quota system.

Few women in the modern military have received more publicity than Kelly J. Flinn has. She made headlines good and bad. Flinn was once considered an ideal advertisement for the United States Air Force when it came to recruiting women. In 1989, Flinn entered the Air Force Academy at the age of eighteen. Three years later, she had been selected for flight training. After graduating in the top fifteen percent of her class, she was the first woman chosen to fly the giant eight-engine B-52 bomber. During B-52 training, Flinn was voted "most distinguished." In 1995, she was the subject of an Air Force promotional film. The sky definitely seemed to be the limit for Lieutenant Kelly Flinn.

Flinn's first permanent-duty assignment was Minot Air Force Base in North Dakota. Things soon went bad. One of only a few women in a squadron of 450 people, Flinn became involved in a relationship with a married man. This resulted in major legal problems for her. She was charged with several serious offenses, including failure to obey lawful orders, fraternization with an enlisted man, conduct unbecoming an officer, and making a false statement. If found guilty of the charges in a court-martial, she faced the possibility of nearly ten years in prison.

In May 1997 Kelly Flinn asked to resign her commission as an Air Force officer. Her request for an honorable discharge was rejected. She was forced to settle for a general discharge but was able to avoid a court-martial. What might have been a brilliant military career was over for Kelly Flinn at the age of only twenty-six.

Her case once again renewed all of the arguments against women flying military aircraft. In her fight against the Air Force, Flinn received strong political and media support. Many felt that a double standard existed for men and women. They argued that a man could get away with the same behavior without harm to his career. There had never been any argument about her technical skills or qualifications as a pilot.

Gaining their rightful place hasn't been easy for women who chose to become pilots in the United States armed forces. It's been a difficult struggle, with lots of barriers to overcome. Pioneering female military aviators such as Barbara Rainey, Sally Murphy, Shannon Workman, Kara Hultgreen, Kelly Flinn, and many others helped to pave the way for future generations of American women.

The roles played by women in America's armed forces have changed greatly over the past couple of decades. Today, only nine percent of army positions and one percent of Air Force jobs exclude women. In the navy, submarines and SEAL teams are the only duties off-limits to females. Nearly 200,000 women serve on active duty in America's armed forces. Female cadets make up just over fifteen percent of the enrollment at the three major military academies.

Lieutenant Colonel Laura Richardson is a prime example of a woman in today's military. She plays multiple roles. The thirty-nine-year-old U.S. Army officer is a Black Hawk helicopter pilot. She is married to an Apache helicopter battalion commander and is the mother of a teenage daughter. Several years ago, Richardson served at the White House as Vice President Al Gore's military aide. More recently, she saw duty overseas. During the 2003 war in Iraq, Richardson commanded the 5th Battalion of the 101st Aviation Brigade. Her unit's thirty helicopters ferried infantry troops into battle. In March 2003, the U.S. Army listed 141 women as AH-64 Apache gunship and UH-60 Black Hawk helicopter pilots.

Military aviation, however, means more than just pilots flying sleek jet fighters, helicopters, or even giant B-52 bombers. Pilots still get most of the recognition, but it takes several people working to keep each pilot flying. Women today fill all kinds of aviation positions. They are aircraft controllers, mechanics, crew chiefs, flight engineers, boom operators, dispatchers, and technicians. All are important to the success of the mission. For years, the United States Marines Corps advertised that it was "looking for a few good men." Today the slogan of America's military should be "We're looking for a few good men and women."

BEYOND THE BOUNDARIES

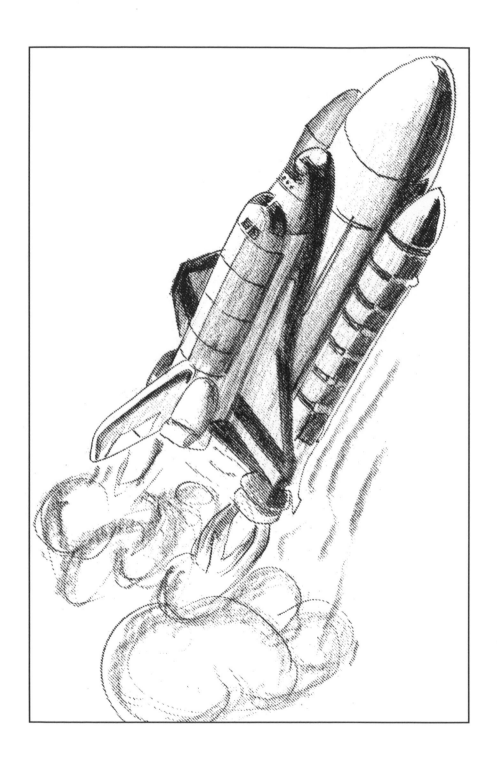

Chapter Seven

Beyond the Boundaries

In its early days, America's space program was run by men—for men only. Nevertheless, many people were working to open up the National Aeronautics and Space Administration's astronaut project to women. Nobody tried harder than Jerrie Cobb did to achieve that goal.

William Cobb gave his daughter, Jerrie, her first flying lesson when she was only twelve. She was hooked! On March 5, 1948, her sixteenth birthday, she passed the test for her pilot's license. Soon after that, she had her commercial license. Learning to fly and getting her licenses were the easy parts, however. Finding a job flying was another matter. Few people were willing to hire a female, let alone a woman as young as Cobb.

She didn't give up. Cobb purchased her own airplane, a surplus Fairchild PT-23, and took every flying job available. She offered lessons and dusted crops. She worked for an oil company, checking pipelines from the air. In 1952, at the age of twenty-one, Jerrie Cobb found a position as an instructor at a flight school. She had plenty of experience. After all, she'd already logged over 2,000 hours of flight time.

The next year, she decided to try her hand at racing. Her first race, the Skylady Derby, covered a distance of 500 miles from Dallas, Texas, to Topeka, Kansas. Cobb came in third. Later that year, she entered the All Women's Transcontinental Race from Santa Ana, California, to Teterboro, New Jersey. Although she had some navigational problems, she finished fourth in the nearly 3,000-mile race.

In 1953, Jerrie Cobb moved to Miami, Florida, where she found a job ferrying airplanes all over the world. Two years later, she was back in the Midwest working as the chief pilot for Executive Aircraft Company in Kansas. On May 25, 1957, she piloted an Aero Commander from Guatemala to Oklahoma City. Cobb set a new speed record when she flew the 1,500-mile distance in slightly over eight hours. That same year, she flew the plane to a height of 30,361 feet and established a new altitude record.

Jerrie Cobb was working as a pilot and manager for Aero Design and Engineering Company of Oklahoma in 1959. Her résumé was impressive. She had more than 7,000 hours of flying experience. She had also set three world aviation records and been awarded the Gold Wings of Achievement by the Fédération Aéronautique Internationale. Then something happened that would turn her life in a new direction.

While on a trip to Miami, Florida, in September 1959, Cobb met W. Randolph Lovelace II. He was the director of a medical facility in Albuquerque, New Mexico, that NASA used to test astronauts. Lovelace suggested that she go through the same evaluation process used to choose the male astronauts for the Mercury 7 project, which had sent the first Americans into space. Naturally, Jerrie Cobb agreed. It seemed to her that Lovelace was offering the impossible. It sounded like a chance to be the first female American astronaut.

A very excited Jerrie Cobb reported to the Lovelace Center on February 14, 1960, to take part in the testing program. Three phases of very intense physical and psychological exams would last for several months. Cobb would be put through all kinds of studies to see if women were as fit as men to be launched into space.

Jerrie Cobb successfully completed the first phase and began the second part of the testing in September 1960. That same month, she flew her Aero Commander to a record-setting altitude of 36,932 feet. On January 25, 1961, the news broke that more women would be allowed to undergo the same testing. Since results based upon only one woman might not be accurate, a bigger pool of candidates was needed. Unlike Cobb, who had been forced to go through the program alone, these women would be evaluated in pairs.

Initial testing for the new group of twelve women would run from January to July 1961. Along with Jerrie Cobb, Bernice Steadman, Jane Hart, Jerri Truhill, Rhea Woltman, Sarah Ratley, Jan Dietrich, Marion Dietrich, Myrtle Cagle, Irene Leverton, Gene Nora Jessen, Jean Hixson, and Wally Funk eventually completed the initial round of tests. The press christened the women "astronettes" and "the Mercury 13." The nicknames were obvious references to NASA's first group of male astronauts.

Meanwhile, Jerrie Cobb had finished the final portion of her testing at the U.S. Naval School of Aviation Medicine in Pensacola, Florida. In June 1961, the National Aeronautics and Space Administration appointed Cobb as a consultant. The experiment seemed to be going well. Cobb's spirits were high. Then, suddenly, it was over. The program was abruptly canceled. Only Wally Funk and Jerrie Cobb had completed the entire evaluation process.

Several reasons were given for the unexpected end of the program. Cobb and the other women weren't satisfied with the answers, however. In an effort to further their cause, they appealed to anyone who would listen. Jane Hart and Jerrie Cobb met with Vice President Lyndon B. Johnson in March 1962 but got nowhere. Cobb lobbied NASA's director for an answer. She worked tirelessly to convince the organization that sending an American woman into space was a good idea. In June, NASA decided not to renew her contract as a consultant.

Jerrie Cobb and Jane Hart were invited to testify before the House Committee on Science and Astronautics in July 1962. This would be their opportunity to tell lawmakers how qualified women were to be part of NASA's space program. It would be their best chance to convince Congress that women were more than able to handle space flight. Jacqueline Cochran, America's most famous woman flier at the time, was also invited to attend the hearings.

Mercury 7 astronauts John Glenn and Scott Carpenter were listed as additional witnesses. They were obviously well qualified to talk about the space program. After all, Glenn and Carpenter had been the first two American astronauts to orbit the Earth. Cochran was no less impressive. Her exploits in the air and her leadership of the WASP program during World War II were legendary.

The committee was composed of nine men and two women. Three days of hearings were scheduled. On July 17, discussions regarding NASA's policies and the requirements for future astronauts began. Cobb and Hart were excited and nervous, but they hoped that the session would be beneficial to their cause. Jerrie Cobb made an impassioned statement about the need to include women in NASA's astronaut training. Jane Hart argued that women were highly qualified and could make real contributions to America's space program. She urged the committee to permit women to go into space immediately.

Unfortunately, the hearings did not offer the opportunity that Cobb, Hart, and the other women wanted. In fact, the results were just the opposite. Neither John Glenn nor Scott Carpenter offered support for including women in astronaut training. Cochran's testimony was lukewarm at best. The hearings adjourned halfway through the second day. The committee decided that future NASA astronauts needed to have a background as test pilots. None of the women in the program were considered to be test pilots. That effectively eliminated them from space travel.

Two months later, *Life* magazine named Jerrie Cobb as one of the top one hundred most influential Americans under the age of forty. Unfortunately, her chance of becoming America's first woman astronaut was over. Sixteen more years would pass before NASA would recruit women into the astronaut program. By the time it finally happened, Cobb and the other Mercury 13 women were too old to be considered.

Jerrie Cobb may not have had the opportunity to fly in space. Nevertheless, she made a tremendous contribution to the involvement of women in aviation, as well as to society in general. After leaving the space program, she spent many years flying medicines and supplies to the needy in remote areas of South and Central America. For her life-saving work, Jerrie Cobb was nominated for the Nobel Peace Prize in 1980.

The first female in space wasn't an American. That honor went to a Russian woman named Valentina Tereshkova. In 1961, the twenty-four-year-old former parachutist applied for cosmonaut training in the Soviet space program. A year later, she was one of four women selected. When the Soviet Union launched its Vostak 6 project on June 16,

1963, Valentina Tereshkova was on board. For nearly seventy-one hours, Tereshkova flew in space. She orbited the Earth forty-five times.

The Soviet Union had beaten the United States when they launched the world's first satellite. They did it again when they sent the first man into space. Now they had put the first woman into space. Once again, the Russians had scored a propaganda victory over the young American space program.

Almost twenty years later, an American woman would finally have the chance to fly in space. In 1977, more than 8,000 people applied for the few precious astronaut-training slots at the National Aeronautics and Space Administration. The following year, NASA's astronaut program accepted thirty-five Americans. Six were women. Sally K. Ride, Margaret Rhea Seddon, Kathryn D. Sullivan, Anna L. Fisher, Judith A. Resnick, and Shannon W. Lucid reported for training in July 1978. Each of the six women held either a doctorate or a medical degree.

With a deafening roar and rumble at 7:33 A.M. on June 18, 1983, STS-7 *Challenger* lifted off its Cape Canaveral launch pad. The Shuttle's mission would be to deploy several communications satellites. For the first time, the spacecraft carried a crew of five. Of greater note, it carried Sally K. Ride, a mission specialist, high above the Earth. An American woman finally had the chance to fly in space.

Aboard *Challenger,* Sally Ride logged six days and over 2.5 million miles in space. Tremendous publicity surrounded her flight. Ride had trained as an astrophysicist, a very complicated and difficult job. Nevertheless, she was quite modest about her selection as the first American woman in space. She said, "I didn't come into this program to be the first woman in space. I came to get a chance to fly."

Another of the first six female astronauts, Judith A. Resnick had her opportunity to fly in space in August 1984. STS-41D was the first mission for the orbiter *Discovery*. Mission specialist Resnick helped to deploy three satellites during a flight that circled Earth ninety-six times and lasted almost 145 hours.

Challenger sat on Kennedy Space Center's pad 39A on the morning of October 5, 1984. The seven-person crew anxiously awaited

liftoff. Every launch made history, but mission STS-41G was something special. For the first time in the history of Shuttle flights, there
would be two women on board. Sally K. Ride had been a member of
the STS-7 crew only a year earlier. Now she would fly again. Kathryn
D. Sullivan would also be on board as a mission specialist. The crew
would be responsible for a satellite deployment as well as numerous
experiments.

During the eight-day mission, Sullivan became the first American
woman to experience the thrill of a space walk, officially known as an
extravehicular activity. She and Commander David Leestma showed
that a satellite could be refueled in space. In 1987, after logging almost
350 hours in space, Sally Ride left NASA. Kathryn Sullivan would
make two more flights and log over 532 hours before leaving the space
program in 1992.

One by one, the first six female NASA astronauts got their chance
to fly in space. Anna L. Fisher's opportunity came on November 8,
1984. On an earlier mission, malfunctioning motors had placed two
satellites in an incorrect orbit. Repairs were needed. First Joseph P.
Allen and Dale A. Gardner captured the satellites during a space walk.
Then Anna Fisher operated the remote manipulator system to maneu-
ver the equipment into the Shuttle's payload bay. On day five of its
192-hour flight, the STS-51A crew completed the first salvage mission
in space history.

The last two women members of the astronaut class of 1978
received their chance to visit space in 1985. Margaret Rhea Seddon
flew on board STS-51D *Discovery* in April 1985. Also on board was
Senator E. J. "Jake" Garn, a participant in the Politicians in Space program. Dr. Seddon served as a mission specialist on STS-51D and STS-
40 and as a payload commander on STS-58. She logged more than 722
hours in space before leaving NASA in 1997.

Nearly a decade after entering the program, the last woman in
NASA's original group of female astronauts finally had her chance to
fly in space. Dr. Shannon W. Lucid was assigned as a mission specialist aboard STS-51G. Her storied career in space was about to begin
with the 7:33 A.M. launch, on June 17, 1985, of America's eighteenth
Shuttle mission. The fifth flight of the Shuttle *Discovery* went off

without a hitch. During the successful seven-day mission, the six-person crew deployed three communications satellites.

Her career with NASA wasn't over yet. Shannon Lucid made four additional flights and spent more than six months living aboard the Russian Space Station MIR. She logged a total of 223 days—not hours, but days—in space. All of that time in space gave Lucid the international record for the most flight hours in orbit by a non-Russian, as well as the record for the most flight hours in orbit by any woman in the world. She is the only woman to receive the Congressional Space Medal of Honor. In February 2002, Dr. Shannon W. Lucid was named as NASA's chief scientist. In that job, she led a three-person council responsible for shaping the future of space exploration.

Nineteen new astronaut candidates entered NASA's astronaut-training program in January 1980. Bonnie J. Dunbar and Mary L. Cleave were the only women selected. Both would get their opportunity to visit space in 1985. As a crewmember of STS-61A *Challenger* on October 30, 1985, Dunbar became the seventh American woman in space. A month later, as part of the STS-61B *Atlantis* mission, Mary Cleave joined that very select group. By 2003, the two women had made a combined total of seven space flights.

Early in 1986, Judith A. Resnick, one of America's six original female astronauts, was scheduled to make her second space flight. STS-51L *Challenger* would be NASA's twenty-fifth Shuttle mission. The very modern and sophisticated orbiter had been named for a British ship that had sailed the Atlantic and Pacific oceans in the 1870s. During its previous nine missions, *Challenger* had spent sixty-nine days in space, orbited the Earth 987 times, and logged millions of miles. The objectives for Resnick's flight included the deployment of Tracking Data Relay Satellite-2 and numerous experiments.

The seven-person STS-51L crew also included another woman. Sharon Christa McAuliffe was making history as the first private American citizen to go into space. In preparation for her flight, she had undergone more than a year of rigorous astronaut training. During the mission, the New Hampshire history and social-studies teacher intended to broadcast televised lessons from space to students back home on Earth. When Christa McAuliffe first applied for NASA's Teacher in

Space program, she wrote, "I watched the Space Age being born and I would like to participate."

The launch of STS-51L had difficulties from the start. Various problems delayed the launch five times. Finally, on January 28, 1986, STS-51L *Challenger* lifted off launch pad 39B at 11:38 A.M. Almost immediately a puff of gray smoke came from the right solid rocket booster. Within seconds, darker puffs of smoke appeared. Then the unthinkable happened. Seventy-three seconds after launch, a massive explosion at an altitude of 46,000 feet destroyed the Shuttle. Huge plumes of white smoke could be seen from hundreds of miles away. Seven lives were lost.

Shuttle launches would not resume until September 1988. Another American woman wouldn't have the chance to fly on board a Shuttle until May 4, 1989. As one of a five-member crew assigned to STS-30, Mary L. Cleave became the first American woman to venture into space since the explosion of *Challenger*.

By the middle of 1992, women had served as crew members on twenty successful launches. Shuttle crews had also included four African-American men—Guion S. Bluford, Ronald McNair, Frederick Gregory, and Charles Bolden. Then, on September 12, 1992, another barrier fell. Dr. Mae C. Jemison became the first African-American woman to venture into space. She flew aboard STS-47 *Endeavour,* a joint venture between the United States and Japan.

Following the launch, the seven-person crew divided into two teams to allow around-the-clock experiments. Each day members of the blue team—Jan Davis, Jay Apt, and Mae Jemison—worked on several projects in the Spacelab-J module. As part of her duties, Jemison also took part in several live television broadcasts. During the shows, she fielded questions from students, teachers, and reporters back on Earth. Six months after her groundbreaking flight, Dr. Mae Jemison left NASA to resume her medical career. By 2003, several female African-American astronauts awaited mission assignments.

Other women were also flying in space again as part of the Shuttle program. On her third mission, Kathryn C. Thornton walked in space for the second time. Several of the female astronauts experienced their second, third, and even fourth launches into space. Shannon Lucid continued to log hours on additional missions. Tremendous accomplishments had been made. Nonetheless, no American woman had served as a Shuttle pilot or Shuttle commander.

United States Air Force officer Eileen M. Collins would change all that. She became a NASA astronaut in 1991. After spending four years in various capacities at NASA, Collins was chosen to be the first female Shuttle pilot. Her chance came with the flawless launch of STS-63 *Discovery* on February 3, 1995. During its successful mission, STS-63 approached and flew around Russian space station MIR. Among her personal belongings, Eileen Collins carried an international pilot's license that had belonged to Bobbi Trout, a pioneering female aviator.

Eight days later, with Eileen Collins at the Shuttle controls, *Discovery* made a perfect landing at Kennedy Space Center. Afterward, she recalled, "I knew all those women pilots out there were watching me and thinking, 'Eileen, you better make a good landing.'" One more barrier had been broken.

In May 1997, Collins had her next opportunity to go into space. She served as pilot of the STS-84 *Atlantis* mission. That flight marked the third time a woman had been at the controls of the Space Shuttle. Susan L. Still had served as pilot for the STS-83 *Columbia* mission one month earlier. There was still more to come, however.

During a gala celebration at the White House in March 1998, First Lady Hillary Rodham Clinton announced, "In December 1998, when the Shuttle *Columbia* takes off, Colonel Eileen Collins will take one big step forward for women and one great leap for humanity." Eileen Collins was going to break down still one more barrier for women. A NASA press release said it all in the first line: "Astronaut Collins will become the first woman to command a Space Shuttle." Eileen Collins didn't get her chance quite as soon as Hillary Rodham Clinton had predicted, but she didn't have long to wait. Collins was named Shuttle commander of the STS-93 *Columbia* mission to deploy the Chandra X-Ray observatory.

On July 20, 1999, Shuttle *Columbia* was ready for liftoff from pad 39B at the Kennedy Space Center. Thousands of NASA employees, visiting celebrities, and enthusiastic spectators were on hand to cheer the launch. Many waved signs of encouragement for Eileen Collins, including one that read, "Eileen—you go, girl!" Hillary Rodham Clinton and her daughter, Chelsea, were in the audience. Sally Ride, America's first woman in space, and the entire United States women's soccer team were there as well.

Less than seven seconds before launch, the mission was delayed by a dangerous buildup of hydrogen in the Shuttle's engine department. A controller shouted, "Cutoff!" The crew quickly shut down Shuttle systems. Two days later, bad weather postponed the flight a second time. Finally, on July 23, 1999, STS-93 lifted off successfully. Regarding her third mission and her first as commander, Eileen Collins said, "I am confident to handle anything." Hillary Rodham Clinton had been right. It was one big step forward for women!

NASA's 113th Shuttle flight was scheduled for January 16, 2003. Shuttle launches had become routine. Americans barely paid attention to them. STS-107 *Columbia* had received press coverage only because of one of its seven crew members, Ilan Ramon, was Israel's first astronaut. The other six astronauts—Rich Husband, Kalpana Chawla, David Brown, William McCool, Michael Anderson, and Laurel Clark—weren't familiar to most people. Even the fact that Kalpana Chawla and Laurel Clark were both women wasn't cause for excitement.

Liftoff seemed to go without a hitch, except for one thing that seemed unimportant at the time. On launch, a piece of insulating foam from an external fuel tank broke off. The foam appeared to hit the Shuttle's left wing, but NASA believed the Shuttle to be undamaged. During the sixteen-day mission, the crew was busy around the clock. Two teams of astronauts worked twelve hours each day to complete nearly one hundred scientific experiments.

On the morning of February 1, the STS-107 mission was coming to an end. *Columbia* reentered the Earth's atmosphere, headed for Florida's Kennedy Space Center at an altitude of 200,700 feet. The Shuttle was traveling at a speed of 12,500 miles per hour. Everything seemed to be on target for a successful landing. Touchdown was scheduled for sixteen minutes later.

Then mission control noticed a problem with *Columbia*'s temperature gauges. Contact with the Shuttle was unexpectedly lost at 9 A.M.

Controllers declared an emergency. As *Columbia* hurtled through the atmosphere, the Shuttle began to disintegrate. People in Texas, Louisiana, and Arkansas heard loud booms and felt the ground shake. Plumes of smoke trailed behind as the Shuttle broke into pieces. Keen-eyed observers on the ground watched the trails of destruction in the sky.

The twenty-eighth flight of *Columbia* had ended in the death of seven crew members. President George W. Bush spoke to a stunned nation only hours after the tragedy. He told the world, "The *Columbia's* lost. There are no survivors." Future missions were post-poned indefinitely until the cause of the disaster could be determined and corrected. The astronauts had not died in vain, however. NASA promised that America's exploration of the universe would continue.

Since Sally Ride's epic venture into space in 1983, women have become a vital part of America's space program. Nearly forty have flown as crew members on Shuttle missions. They have served as Shuttle pilots and commanders. Several American women have lived aboard space stations. Others have had the chance to walk in space. At the beginning of the twenty-first century, women comprised nearly twenty-five percent of NASA's astronaut program.

If there were only astronauts, however, space exploration would never take place. Thousands of people, both male and female, labor behind the scenes to make America's space program successful. At the National Aeronautics and Space Administration, women make up approximately one-third of the total work force. Women hold key positions such as chief scientist, project manager, chief mission engi-neer, project scientist, launch commentator, and flight director. They are just more examples of the roles women have played in aviation. They help America's space program go beyond the boundaries.

CHESS
MOVE BY MOVE

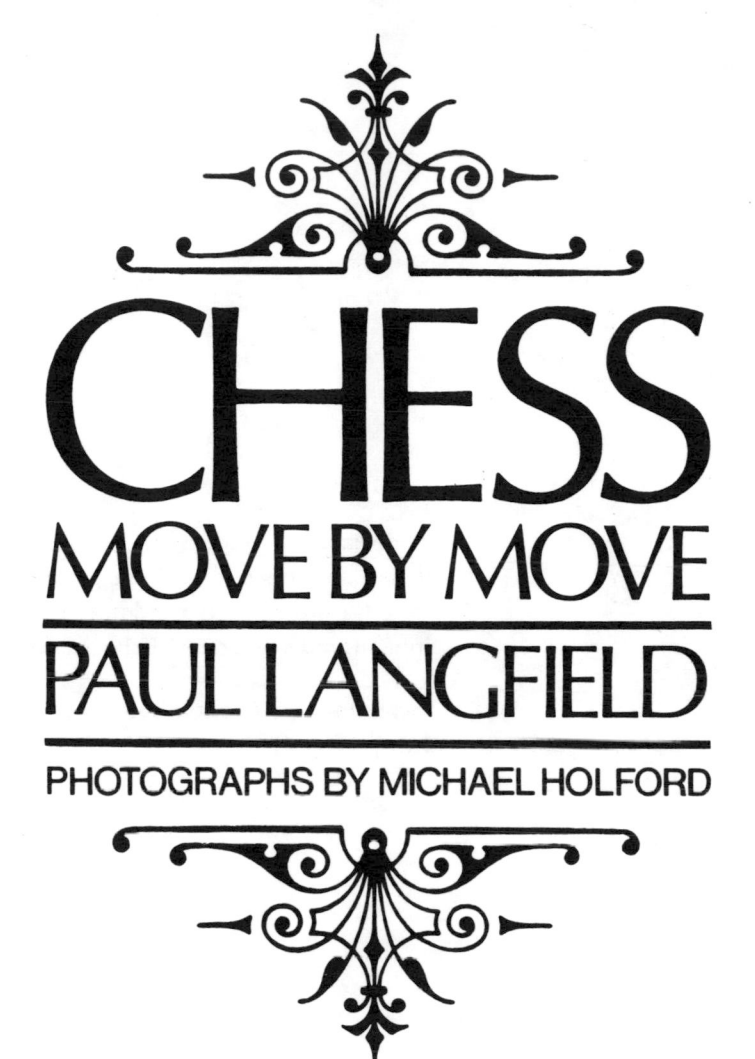

CHESS
MOVE BY MOVE
PAUL LANGFIELD

PHOTOGRAPHS BY MICHAEL HOLFORD

HAMLYN

LONDON · NEW YORK · SYDNEY · TORONTO

'I declare it's marked out just like a large chessboard!' Alice said at last ... 'It's a great huge game of chess that's being played—all over the world ... I wouldn't mind being a Pawn, if only I might join—though of course I should *like* to be a Queen, best.'

THROUGH THE LOOKING-GLASS
Lewis Carroll

Second Impression, 1970
Third Impression, 1971
Fourth Impression, 1972
Fifth Impression, 1972
Sixth Impression, 1973
Seventh Impression, 1974
Eighth Impression, 1975

ISBN 0 600 40040 9
Published by
THE HAMLYN PUBLISHING GROUP LIMITED
LONDON - NEW YORK - SYDNEY - TORONTO
Astronaut House, Feltham, Middlesex, England
Printed in England by Butler and Tanner Limited, Frome and London.

For Shelagh Margaret with love

CONTENTS

The author and publishers would like to express their grateful thanks to A. E. J. Mackett-Beeson for his generous help in lending them the beautiful chess pieces illustrated in this book

FOREWORD

Before learning how to play chess the reader may like to know a little about the historical background of the game. Many knowledgable authorities have done a great deal of research in this field but, alas, there is often much in their findings which is contradictory.

No one can state, with any real certainty, the date of origin of the game because the early history of chess is not only lost in antiquity but confused by intriguing myth and legend. Some authorities claim that it was invented by the Hindus on the banks of the Ganges some three thousand years prior to the 6th century. On the other hand, one of Britain's foremost international masters, Harry Golombek, in *The Game of Chess*, gives the 5th century as the probable period of the origins of the game. Nearly all modern authorities agree that the credit for inventing the game must go to the Hindus and that it was then called *chaturanga*, meaning four *angas* or members of an army.

The intention of the game was to symbolise an imaginary battle between Indian armies. Pieces were created to imitate, as closely as possible, the four divisions of an army—elephants, horses, chariots and foot soldiers—headed, of course, by a king. The Queen in the original game was a male and is thought to have been a 'minister' or 'general'. It was not until the game reached Europe that the Piece changed sex and this adjustment was attributed to the French.

Among the existing myths and legends are references to chess having been invented by Arabians, Babylonians, Chinese, Egyptians, Jews, Persians and even the Irish and Welsh. Modern research has shown these theories to be ill founded. Earlier historians, with very little authority, gave credit for the invention of the game to many and diverse historical characters, including King Solomon, the philosophers Xerxes and Aristotle, as well as various lesser-known personalities.

Chaturanga differed from the game we play today as it was originally devised for four players and the moves were determined by

9

casting a dice. Early in the 6th century considerable changes in the method of play took place as the Moslem law forbade all forms of gambling and the use of dice had to be discarded so the game was then confined to only two players. At about the same time *chaturanga* was introduced into Persia, by Indian ambassadors appointed to the Persian court, where it was called *chatrang*. In the 7th century Persia was invaded and captured by the Arabs, whose alphabet included neither the first nor the final letter of the word, and the term they used was *shatranj*, which name in due course found its way into the modern Persian language.

From this phase on authorities differ in their accounts of the passage of the game from one country to another, but most agree that the probable entry into Europe was from Italy and Spain. The Italians almost certainly learnt from the Byzantines, and the Spanish from their Moslem conquerors. It is probable that the game travelled northwards to France and in due course on to Scandinavia and Great Britain. There is a theory that Christian warriors returning from the Crusades brought back chess with them but there is little evidence to substantiate this.

Few changes were made in the game until about the middle of the 15th century when the Queen, who was then one of the weakest pieces on the board, was given the dominating power she holds today. Instead of being confined to moving one square at a time, and that diagonally, she had all the privileges conferred upon her which are described on pages 22/23.

Another important change in the rules took place about one hundred years later. During the 16th century 'castling' was introduced—a move you will learn about later—and the Pawn's first move was no longer confined to one square forward but could now be advanced two squares if the player so desired. Both these changes were European innovations. No other major change in the rules has been introduced since then and the game played in the 16th century is basically the same as that played at the present time and explained in this book.

INTRODUCTION

You do not have to be clever to play chess. It is, of course, a game of skill but provided that you know the rules then you can play. This holds good for any player from a six-year-old to an octogenarian.

Ask your friends if they play chess. If they do, nine out of ten will reply that they 'know the moves'. This may, of course, be modesty and perhaps they are very good players. On the other hand, it may be the truth. To be a good player you must not only know the moves but you must make good use of the Pieces you are moving. The more you play, the better you become.

If you do not play and you have the opportunity to watch a game in progress you will very soon be baffled. The various Pieces moved across the board seem to be governed by many different and unpredictable rules and there seems to be no rhyme or reason in any of it. However, if you take the Pieces separately and practise the moves they can make, it soon becomes a clear and logical game. You need a set of chessmen and a board. Once you have acquired these you have only to read this book and practise the moves and you will be playing chess in no time at all.

You cannot expect to be good in your first game. But you will quickly learn from your mistakes and with each game played your skill should increase.

It is useful to have an opponent when learning but if none is available you can always play against yourself by turning the board after each move. This way you should be able to force yourself to a draw! Any child of six, or in some cases younger, can learn the game. With this in mind the moves have been described as simply as possible and I have assumed that the reader knows absolutely nothing at all about the game. Younger children will need the aid of a parent as well as the book but the older child will find nothing here that he cannot master on his own.

It should be pointed out, however, that although the photographs in this book illustrate some of the beautiful and rare chess pieces in existence today, chess is usually played with the Staunton pieces as shown in the jacket photograph and on page 53.

Finally let me say that I have three young daughters all of whom now play a fiercely competitive game of chess. They all learned by the easy step-by-step method described here and the notes and diagrams I compiled for them at the time later formed the basis for the first part of this book.

PART ONE

HOW TO PLAY

THE GAME

1 The board. Note the white square at the right corner for each player

The Board

If you turn to the numbered board on pages 26/27, you will see that there are sixty-four squares of which thirty-two are White and the other thirty-two are Black.

Before you set up the Pieces for a game always make sure that the square in the near right-hand corner of your board is White *(Fig. 1)*. This will automatically be the same for your opponent. If by mischance you start the game with the board the wrong way round you should stop and set up the Pieces again.

The squares which run in lines from the north to south as shown in *Fig. 2* are the Files. The squares which go from left to right across the board as shown in *Fig. 3* are the Ranks. Some Pieces, as we shall see later, can be moved across diagonals—that is across the corners of the squares. *Figs. 4 and 5* show the diagonals. The chessboard in this book is numbered but the

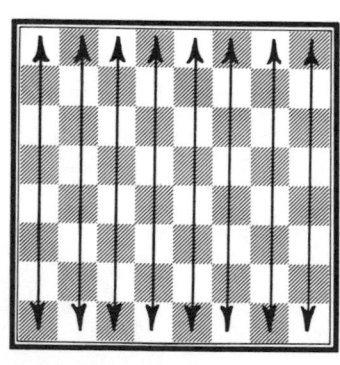

2 The Files are the rows of squares which go towards and away from your opponent

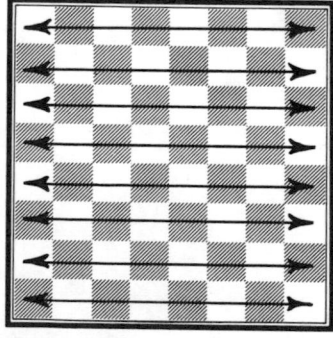

3 The Ranks are the rows of squares going from left to right and right to left across the board

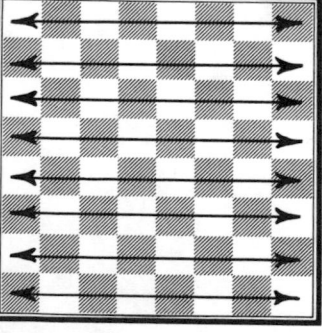

4 Diagonals are the paths running across the corners of the squares

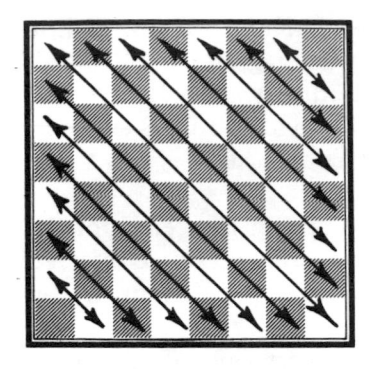

5 Diagonals

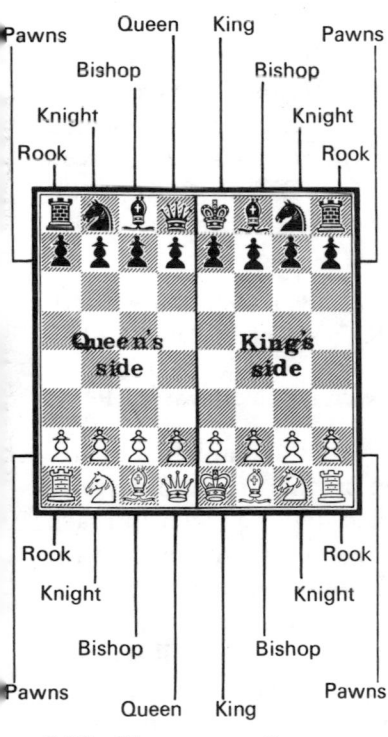

6 The Pieces set out for a game

board you will play on is not. The numbering is there for two reasons; first of all it helps you to learn how to play, and later on you will find it useful if you want to play out a game which has been played by others and all the moves have been recorded.

At first glance the numbering may look complicated but it is really quite simple. In any case, you do not have to memorise the numbers, but to be able to use the board you will have to know the simple system of numbering. Before we tackle this let us learn the names of the Pieces, and for simplicity we will start from the bottom left-hand corner of the board.

The Pieces

Look at *Fig. 6*. In the bottom left-hand corner is a little castle standing on a Black square. This is a Rook, although it is sometimes called a Castle. You will find four Pieces like this in your set—two White and two Black.

The movements of the Rook are clearly set forth in the next chapter, but for the moment we are concerned only with the position in which it starts and any other square on which it might find itself during the course of the game.

The Rook starts on QR 1 on the left of the board and KR 1 on the right for the White Pieces and the other way round for the Black Pieces. Q stands for Queen and K for King.

In the centre of the starting row you will see a Queen and a King. All Pieces standing on the Queen's side are the Queen's Pieces and, as you would expect, all those on the other side are King's Pieces.

Look at *Fig. 6* again. Next to the Queen's Rook is a Piece shown as the head of a horse. This is the Queen's Knight and in the same position on the other side of the board is the King's Knight. These two are abbreviated to QKt and KKt. In each case the starting position is QKt 1 and KKt 1. Now look for these on your numbered board on pages 26/27 of the book. Note that the Knight's squares are all numbered 1 in the starting position either for White or Black. The same applies to the numbering for all the other Pieces.

Look again at *Fig. 6*. Moving to the centre of the

starting line we find that each Knight has a Bishop next to him. The symbol on our diagrams is a Bishop's mitre. These are respectively the Queen's Bishop and the King's Bishop and are abbreviated to QB and KB. As you would expect the starting square is QB 1 and KB 1.

Between the two Bishops and in the centre of the first Rank are the Queen and King. These are referred to as Q and K and in their starting positions are on squares Q 1 and K 1.

Note that the White Queen starts on a White square whereas the Black Queen is opposite her and starts on a Black square. The easy way to remember this when setting up the Pieces is that the Queen always starts on a square of her own colour.

It helps to think of all these Pieces on the first Rank as striking Pieces, although the Pawns also have power to take as we shall see later. Each Pawn is named according to the Piece it stands in front of and you have a King Pawn, Queen Pawn, two Bishop Pawns, two Knight Pawns and two Rook Pawns. These are abbreviated as follows:

Queen Pawn QP	Queen's Knight Pawn QKtP
King Pawn KP	King's Knight Pawn KKtP
Queen's Bishop Pawn QBP	Queen's Rook Pawn QRP
King's Bishop Pawn KBP	King's Rook Pawn KRP

Now look again at both *Fig. 6* and the numbered board. The striking Pieces all start on the firs• number of a File of squares. In front of each stands a Pawn and each of these is on a number 2 of the File. If it moves forward one square at a time each Pawn eventually arrives at its own number 8 square. This, of course, is the number 1 square of your opponent. You will see that the numbers for both players have been inserted in the squares. You do *not* have to memorise these numbers and knowing them will not help you at all when you are playing a game. They are useful only because if you know them you can read chess games with them or work out the solutions to chess puzzles.

The game is played visually and the moves are made according to the positions the various Pieces are seen to occupy. On the other hand if you wish to record a

Modern Chinese chess set with lacquer chessboard

game you will have to use the numbering of the various squares.

Other symbols you should know for reading or recording a game are as follows:

— indicates 'move to'
X indicates that a Piece 'takes' another Piece
Ch indicates 'Check'
O.O. means 'Castles' on King's side
O.O.O. means 'Castles' on Queen's side
! means a very good move
? means a poor move

You will want to refer back to these symbols later and we will see what the various moves are in the following chapter.

For the moment let us see what values the various Pieces are said to have.

Value of the Pieces

Remember that Alice in *Through the Looking Glass* said, 'I wouldn't mind being a Pawn . . . though of course I should *like* to be a Queen, best.' Certainly the Queen is the strongest Piece on the board and she should be moved with great care to avoid capture by an enemy Piece. Least powerful, but not to be despised, is the Pawn. Experts give the following values based on one point to a Pawn:

Queen	9 points	Knight	3 points
Rook	5 points		
Bishop	3 points	Pawn	1 point

It is not necessary to remember these figures but we should keep in mind the approximate values of the Pieces especially when we are faced with losing any of them. Fight hard to keep your Queen on the board and do not lightly say 'goodbye' to your Rooks. Bishops and Knights are equal and, although Pawns are the least powerful Pieces, you should not give them away.

Of course the real value of all Pieces depends upon their position on the board at the time you are about to make a move.

The Aim of the Game

The draughts player would do well to forget all about the rules of draughts before he tackles chess. Both

Chinese ball-mounted chess set with hardwood chessboard

games are played on the same board but that is about all that they have in common.

The aim of the chess player is to capture his opponent's King. This does not mean the removal of the King from the board, but simply that the player has so placed his Pieces that his opponent's King is under fire and cannot escape. This is called Checkmate and means that the game is over.

When the game starts both Kings are safely placed behind their Pawns, and on each side of them are striking Pieces which, as we have already seen, are of different values. The strength of these Pieces, as we shall see in the chapter on THE MOVES, is limited by the movements they are allowed to make, but they all have the power to attack the enemy King.

If a piece is so placed on the board that in its next move it could *take* the hostile King it is said to have the King in Check and it is usual for the player to announce this as he makes the move.

The King who is attacked must now do one of four things if the game is to proceed. He must:

1 Move to a square where he is not under attack. It therefore follows that at no stage in the game may a King put himself in Check.
2 He must take the Piece attacking him by moving onto the square from which the attack comes. This he can only do if the attack comes from a square adjacent to the one he is on because a King moves only one square at a time.
3 He must call to his aid one of his own Pieces which can remove the attacking Piece from the board.
4 He must call to his aid one of his own Pieces which can be placed between the attacking Piece and himself.

If any of these moves can be made the King is no longer in Check and the game can proceed.

On the other hand if the King is in Check and in his next move would be moving into Check from another Piece, then he is Checkmated and the game is over. We will discuss moves which Checkmate the King in more detail later.

THE MOVES

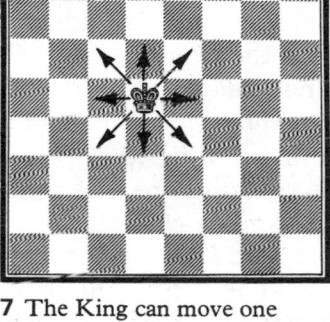

7 The King can move one square only but in any direction

The King

The most important Piece on the board but *not* the most powerful is the King. He must be protected from attack at all times and in particular from being forced into a position from which he cannot escape.

The King is limited in his movements to one square at a time. He can move along Ranks or Files or he can move diagonally across the squares.

Look at *Fig. 7* which shows the Black King on a White square and the arrows indicate the eight squares to any one of which he can move from this particular position. But remember he can travel to only one in each move. If the King is on one of the squares at the edge of the board he is limited to five choices of alternative squares in his next move. If he is in a corner there are only three squares available to him and this is assuming they are not occupied by any of his own Pieces.

Why would the King want to move? You know that if your opponent calls Check you must either remove the Piece which is attacking your King, place one of your other Pieces between your opponent's attacking Piece and your King, or *move your King*.

A King must never move onto a square which is adjacent to the square occupied by the hostile King. There must always be a square between them though this does not have to be vacant. It may be occupied by a Piece belonging to either player.

KING

1 The most important Piece on the board but *not* the most powerful.

2 Moves only one square at a time, except when the player decides to Castle (see pages 33–34).

3 Can move in any direction—along Ranks, up Files, across diagonals, forwards or backwards.

4 Must never move *into* Check—the player must not place his King on any square at which his opponent's striking Pieces are already firing.

5 Must never occupy a square immediately adjoining that of the enemy King.

6 Must constantly be guarded against attack.

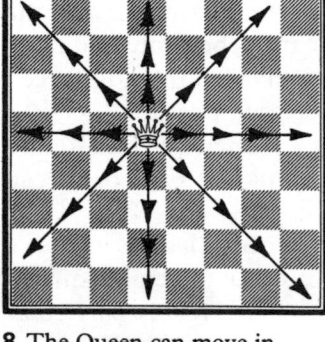

8 The Queen can move in any direction and as far as she likes. She can take an enemy Piece on any of the squares in her path but she must remain on that square until she is moved

The Queen

Next to the King the most important and certainly the most powerful Piece you have is the Queen. And so is your opponent's Queen. We now know that both the striking Pieces and the Pawns can take our opponent's Pieces and we would do well to watch for any opportunity to take our opponent's Queen. If he is a good player we will not be given very much chance.

What are the Queen's moves and how can she take enemy Pieces? Look at *Fig. 8*. The White Queen is placed on Q 5. From this particular square she can strike out in the directions indicated and she can stop and capture—if the particular square is occupied—on any of the squares in which there is an arrow.

From this diagram it will be seen that the Queen can move as far across the board as she wishes provided the way is clear and that no squares in her path are occupied by either Black or White Pieces; she can move along Ranks or Files and also if she wishes she can move diagonally—that is across the corners of the squares. In other words, the Queen can move any distance in any direction but she cannot hop over other Pieces and she cannot change direction in any one move.

Take care in moving your Queen. There is little point in capturing an enemy Pawn if your Queen is taken in the next move by one of your opponent's Pieces.

QUEEN

1 The most powerful Piece on the board.

2 Can move in any direction, along Ranks, up

Files, across diagonals, forwards or backwards.

3 Can move as many squares in any one direction as the player chooses. She must not change direction in any one move.

4 Can capture any enemy Piece on the path she is moving along and must then remain on that square until moved again—or captured!

5 Cannot hop over any Pieces.

6 Must constantly be guarded against attack.

Place a Queen on an empty board and move her across it as described. Place Pawns of the opposite colour in various squares and capture them. Remember the Queen must not move from the Rank, File or diagonal in any one move. See *Fig. 9*. It would need two moves for the Queen to take the Pawn though there is a choice of paths she can take to achieve this. See *Figs. 10 and 11*. There are other paths she can use to take the Pawn. See if you can work them out.

9 White Queen needs two moves to take Black Pawn

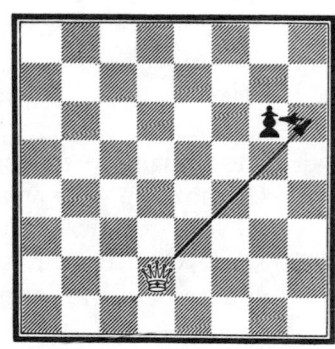

10 The arrows show how the Queen takes this Pawn in two moves

11 Two moves for Queen to take Pawn but by different paths from those shown in Fig. 10

Why do we concern ourselves with more than one route for the Queen? The answer is, of course, that if enemy Pieces are so placed that they can take the Queen after she has moved, she must find some other and safer way to reach her quarry.

The Bishops

The moves of the Bishops are quite simple, in fact the Bishop is confined entirely to diagonals. That is to

23

say he must always move across the corners of the squares. He can advance or retreat and, provided the path is clear, he can go as far as he likes in one move. Look at *Fig. 6* again. You will see that each player has two Bishops. Notice that one of your Bishops starts on a White square and the other starts on Black. Throughout the whole game—or for as long as they remain on the board—they will stay on the colour on which they started.

Bishops cannot jump over Pieces but they can capture any enemy Piece which is on the track they elect to travel along. Having taken a Piece, the Bishop remains on that square until the next time he is moved. If a Bishop is in direct line to an opponent's King and there is no other Piece on that diagonal, he has put the King in Check.

BISHOPS

1 Are confined to diagonals only. They always move across the corners of squares.
2 Can move as far as they like provided the way is clear.
3 Can capture any enemy Piece on the path chosen and remain on that square until moved again.
4 Cannot hop over any Pieces.
5 Always remain on the colour on which they start. One Bishop starts and ends on White squares and the other on Black squares.

Place the White Bishops on the board and remember to put one on a White square and the other on Black. Now place Black Pawns on various squares and see how many moves it takes to clear the board of them.

Fig. 12 shows the Bishop's move. It is Black's turn and in one move the Bishop travels across the corners of the squares to the square occupied by the White Pawn. The White Pawn is now removed and the Bishop stands on this square until he is moved again, or taken by your opponent's Piece.

Fig. 13 shows how the Black Bishop needs two moves to capture the White Pawn. An alternative route is shown in *Fig. 14*. There are other routes but

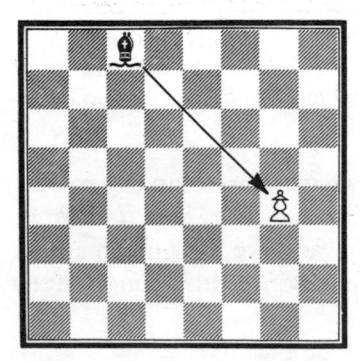

12 Black Bishop takes White Pawn in one move, as shown by arrow

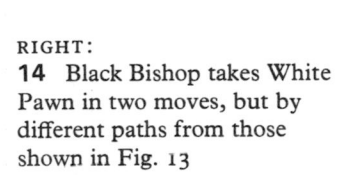

LEFT:

13 Black Bishop needs two moves to take White Pawn from this position

RIGHT:

14 Black Bishop takes White Pawn in two moves, but by different paths from those shown in Fig. 13

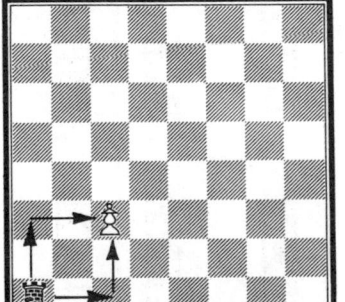

15 White Rook can take Black Pawn in one move, as shown

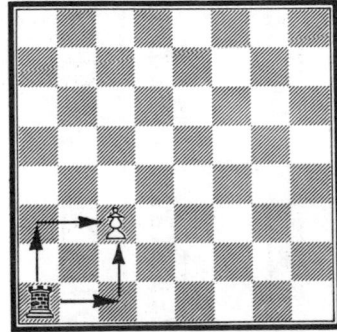

16 Black Rook needs two moves to take White Pawn. He can take either of the two routes shown

they would all require more than two moves to take the Pawn. Try it for yourself.

It would be logical to discuss the Knight's moves next but, as this Piece has a slightly awkward method of progress which makes it different from the other striking Pieces, it is reasonable to leave it for the moment and investigate the moves of the Rook.

The Rooks

Look at *Figs. 2 and 3* again. The squares from left to right of the board are the Ranks and the pathways of squares leading to your opponent's Pieces are the Files. Once this is clear in your mind it is sufficient to remember that Rooks move along Ranks and Files. They never move diagonally like the Bishops.

A Rook can move over as many squares as he likes in one move but he must keep to either a Rank or File. He cannot jump over Pieces. If he is to take a hostile Piece he moves to the square occupied by that Piece which is then removed from the board.

Look at *Fig. 15*. The White Rook can take the Black Pawn in one move.

Now look at *Fig. 16*. If it is Black's turn to move and he aims to take the White Pawn he can only do so in two moves.

First he moves to either of the squares indicated by the arrows and then in his next move he occupies the square on which the White Pawn stands. Remember that players move alternately and, after Black has moved to the striking position, White may decide to move the threatened Piece out of danger.

25

A chessboard diagram in descriptive notation. Each square shows its White designation and its Black designation.

QR	QKt	QB	Q	K	KB	KKt	KR
QR1 / QR8	QKt1 / QKt8	QB1 / QB8	Q1 / Q8	K1 / K8	KB1 / KB8	KKt1 / KKt8	KR1 / KR8
QR2 / QR7	QKt2 / QKt7	QB2 / QB7	Q2 / Q7	K2 / K7	KB2 / KB7	KKt2 / KKt7	KR2 / KR7
QR3 / QR6	QKt3 / QKt6	QB3 / QB6	Q3 / Q6	K3 / K6	KB3 / KB6	KKt3 / KKt6	KR3 / KR6
QR4 / QR5	QKt4 / QKt5	QB4 / QB5	Q4 / Q5	K4 / K5	KB4 / KB5	KKt4 / KKt5	KR4 / KR5
QR5 / QR4	QKt5 / QKt4	QB5 / QB4	Q5 / Q4	K5 / K4	KB5 / KB4	KKt5 / KKt4	KR5 / KR4
QR6 / QR3	QKt6 / QKt3	QB6 / QB3	Q6 / Q3	K6 / K3	KB6 / KB3	KKt6 / KKt3	KR6 / KR3
QR7 / QR2	QKt7 / QKt2	QB7 / QB2	Q7 / Q2	K7 / K2	KB7 / KB2	KKt7 / KKt2	KR7 / KR2
QR8 / QR1	QKt8 / QKt1	QB8 / QB1	Q8 / Q1	K8 / K1	KB8 / KB1	KKt8 / KKt1	KR8 / KR1

WHITE

Descriptive-notation reference board (each square shows its White name and, inverted, its Black name):

KR	KKt	KB	K	Q	QB	QKt	QR
KR1 / KR8	KKt1 / KKt8	KB1 / KB8	K1 / K8	Q1 / Q8	QB1 / QB8	QKt1 / QKt8	QR1 / QR8
KR2 / KR7	KKt2 / KKt7	KB2 / KB7	K2 / K7	Q2 / Q7	QB2 / QB7	QKt2 / QKt7	QR2 / QR7
KR3 / KR6	KKt3 / KKt6	KB3 / KB6	K3 / K6	Q3 / Q6	QB3 / QB6	QKt3 / QKt6	QR3 / QR6
KR4 / KR5	KKt4 / KKt5	KB4 / KB5	K4 / K5	Q4 / Q5	QB4 / QB5	QKt4 / QKt5	QR4 / QR5
KR5 / KR4	KKt5 / KKt4	KB5 / KB4	K5 / K4	Q5 / Q4	QB5 / QB4	QKt5 / QKt4	QR5 / QR4
KR6 / KR3	KKt6 / KKt3	KB6 / KB3	K6 / K3	Q6 / Q3	QB6 / QB3	QKt6 / QKt3	QR6 / QR3
KR7 / KR2	KKt7 / KKt2	KB7 / KB2	K7 / K2	Q7 / Q2	QB7 / QB2	QKt7 / QKt2	QR7 / QR2
KR8 / KR1	KKt8 / KKt1	KB8 / KB1	K8 / K1	Q8 / Q1	QB8 / QB1	QKt8 / QKt1	QR8 / QR1

17 How many moves for Black Rook to take all the Pawns?

Place a Black Rook on your board as shown in *Fig. 17* with the White Pawns placed as shown in the diagram. Ignore the fact that in a real game you would have an opponent who makes a move every time you do but just practise mopping up the Pawns by using your Rook correctly.

ROOKS

1 Are confined to Ranks and Files. They cannot use diagonals.
2 Can move forwards or backwards as far as they like provided the way is clear.
3 Can capture any enemy Piece on the path chosen and remain on that square until moved again.
4 Cannot hop over any Pieces.
5 Are second only to the Queen in power and should be moved with great care.

We will see later on how Rooks working together can achieve a Checkmate. In the meantime let us see what the Knights can do.

The Knights

None of the moves we have so far discussed has been difficult to learn. The Knight's move is no exception but it does present difficulties to the writer who tries to explain it to a beginner. I have heard it described as a jump from one corner of a six-squared rectangle to the opposite corner. This is true but it is not the easiest way to learn the move. A better approach is to simplify the move by thinking of it as two squares in one direction and one square in another direction all in the same move. Alternatively one square in one direction and two squares in another direction all in the same move.

The Knight is the only Piece on the board which can hop over another Piece to arrive at its destination. The Piece it hops over can be either one of the player's own Pieces or one belonging to his opponent.

Note that the Knight does *not* take the Piece it hops over but it does capture any Piece on the square it lands on. It therefore follows that a Knight is never moved to a square occupied by one of the player's own Pieces.

18 White Knight can take Black Pawn in one move

Like the other striking Pieces the Knight can move backwards or forwards across the board but his move must be confined to two squares in one direction and one square in another making an L-shape.

Look at *Fig. 18*. The White Knight here is in his starting position and from this square he can take the Black Pawn in one move. *Fig. 19* shows the move—two squares up the File and one square along the Rank. One square to the right and two up the File would bring the Knight to the same destination.

Now look at *Fig. 20* and you will see that the Black Knight is surrounded by Pawns. He can capture any one Pawn in one move. *Figs. 21–23* show how three Pawns can be taken from this position. Work out the others on your board and you will soon have mastered the Knight's move.

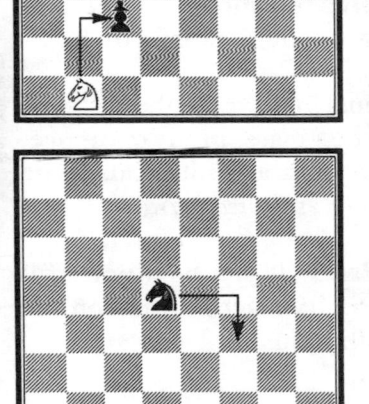

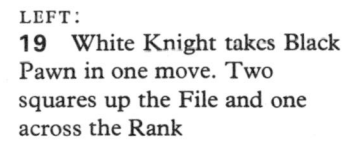

LEFT:
19 White Knight takes Black Pawn in one move. Two squares up the File and one across the Rank

RIGHT:
20 Black Knight can take any one of these White Pawns in his next move

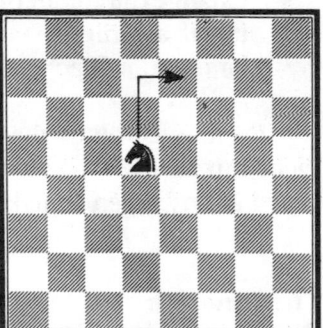

21 Black Knight moves two squares across the Rank and then one square down the File to capture a Pawn in one move

22 In this move Black Knight moves up the File two squares and then one square across the Rank

23 From the same position Black Knight makes another L-shaped move. Look at Fig. 20 again and note that there were Pawns on all the squares to which Black Knight had moved

Note that a Knight, when moved, starts on a square of one colour but always completes the move by arriving on a square of the other colour.

A Knight can be moved to every square on the board. Try it out by placing pennies, buttons or bits of paper on all the squares and remove each one as the Knight lands on that particular square. It is a good way to practise the Knight's move.

Remember that the Knight must always make this complete L-shaped move of two squares in a Rank and one along a File, or one square along the Rank and two in the File, and he cannot stop after just one or two squares.

KNIGHTS

1 Are the only Pieces which can change direction in one move.
2 Are the only Pieces which *can* hop over other Pieces—your own or your opponent's.
3 Are limited in any one move to going forward or backwards two squares and then one square to the side. Alternatively, the move can be two squares to the side and one forwards or backwards.
4 Are approximately equal in power to the Bishops.
5 Change the colour of the squares in any one move, i.e. if a Knight starts from a White square, he lands on a Black square and *vice versa*.

We now come to the Pawn. It can be a powerful Piece but this will depend on its exact position on the board at any given time in the game.

24 White moves Queen's Pawn two squares in his first move

The Pawns

The movement of the Pawn is quite simple. It goes forward towards the opponent's Pieces one square at a time in its own File. A Pawn can move two squares forward in its first move but this is optional. Thereafter it is confined to one square at a time.

Look at *Fig. 24*. The Black Pieces have been removed from the board to avoid confusion and White

25 White moves another square forward towards his opponent

has made his first move. He has moved his Queen's Pawn two places forward exercising the option we have mentioned. Now look at *Fig. 25*.

PAWNS

1 The least powerful Pieces on the board but they should always be moved with care.
2 Move one square at a time except when they make their first move and the player has the option of moving them two places forward.
3 Always move forward in their own Files. They never retreat.
4 Always take opponent's Pieces diagonally. Only then do they change Files.
5 Never hop over other Pieces.
6 Cannot move forward if there is a Piece of either colour on the square immediately in front of them. They are then 'blocked'.

White has moved one square forward and is only three squares from his opponent's back row. *Figs. 26 and 27* show his next moves and you will see that he proceeds doggedly on, one square at a time. Now look at *Fig. 28*. White's Pawn has reached its destination and has turned into a Queen!

26 White Pawn goes forward another square, keeping to his own File

27 White Pawn is now only one square from Black's back Rank

28 White's Pawn has arrived at Black's back Rank and has changed into another Queen!

We have already seen that a Queen is the strongest Piece on the board so obviously this achievement is well worth aiming for.

31

Alas, it is not so easy to gain a Queen as the diagrams suggest. When your opponent's Pieces are on the board and he makes a move after each of your moves, one or other of his Pieces will make short work of your over-ambitious Pawn.

It should be stated that when a Pawn has reached an opponent's back row the player can exchange it for any other Piece, except a King. Most chess sets contain only one Queen for each player so you may be faced with a problem if you succeed in getting one of your Pawns to your opponent's back row. It is usual to make a Queen by placing a Pawn on top of a Rook if there is one off the board at the time. Or you might try balancing one Pawn on top of another. But first Queen your Pawn!

Pawns can, of course, take other Pieces and they can put a King in Check. It is important to remember that Pawns take hostile Pieces diagonally. Although it moves in its own File, the Pawn changes File when it occupies the square of an enemy Piece it has taken.

Look at *Fig. 29*. White has made his first move and it is Queen's Pawn to Q 4. Because it is the Pawn's first move it has gone forward two squares.

Now Black replies and *Fig. 30* shows he has elected to move his King's Pawn and he, too, has used the rule which allows the Pawn two squares in its first move. This was not a good move.

It is White's turn so White Pawn now takes Black Pawn and occupies the square formerly held by Black as shown in *Fig. 31*.

29 White opens with Queen's Pawn to Q 4

LEFT:
30 Black's opening move is King's Pawn to K 4

RIGHT:
31 White Pawn takes Black Pawn and occupies the square from which the Black Pawn is removed. Pawns always take diagonally

32 Black moves his Queen's Pawn to Q 4 and blocks his opponent's Pawn. A much better move than that shown in Fig. 30

A better move for Black would have been to block the path of the White Pawn by moving his own Queen's Pawn two squares as shown in *Fig. 32*.

Before taking the game any further you should know that there are two other rules you will have to learn. If you are impatient to get started you can leave this chapter and go straight on to the next one. It is possible to play a game through to Checkmate without using either of the moves which I will now describe.

If you decide to omit this part do not forget to come back to it after you have played your trial game. Otherwise you will one day meet an opponent who Castles when you are not expecting it and you will not know what it is all about.

By the same token he may capture a Pawn of yours in a way you did not know was possible. Let us deal with Castling first.

Castling

This is a move to which each player is entitled and which is made by the player once only in any game. It is the only time the King can travel more than one square in a move and the only time the player changes the position of two of his Pieces in one move. The other Piece involved is the Rook.

If neither King nor Rook have made a move in the game, and if the intervening squares are unoccupied, the player may move his King two squares towards the Rook which is then placed on the other side of the King in the square next to the King as shown in *Fig. 33*. *Fig. 34* shows the move completed on the King's side of the board.

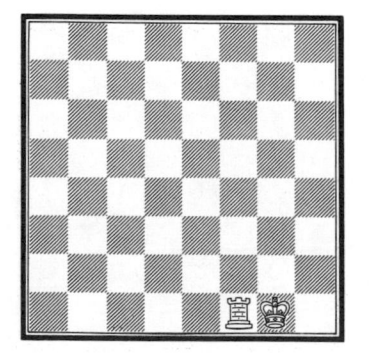

LEFT:
33 White Castles on King's side

RIGHT:
34 The Castling move completed

35 White Castles on the Queen's side

36 The Castling move completed. Note that on the Queen's side there are two squares vacant beyond the King

The same rules apply to Castling on the Queen's side. Note that when this is done there are two squares beyond the King and not one as is the case when the Castling is done on the King's side.

What is the purpose of this move? It is usually twofold. In the first place the King is being moved to a safer position and in the second place the Rook is brought towards the centre of the board to a position where it can be better employed for attacking purposes. This may not always be the case and if a player has not Castled early in the game he should only do so if he sees an advantage in the move.

Remember, you cannot Castle if there are Pieces on the squares between the King and the Rook; if the King or the Rook has already made a move in the game, or if the King is in Check.

The En Passant Rule

You know that a Pawn moves one square forward in all its moves except in the first, when the player has the option of moving it two squares. Suppose that in doing this a Pawn escapes capture from another Pawn, then the Pawn that has been foiled can, in fact, make the capture as if the Pawn first moved had gone forward one square only.

Fig. 37 shows the advancing Black Pawn and it is White's turn. He decides to move his King Bishop's Pawn and because this is the Pawn's first move he advances it two places to bring it alongside the attacking Black Pawn, as shown in *Fig. 38*.

LEFT:
37 The En Passant rule. It is White's turn to move

RIGHT:
38 White moves his King's Bishop Pawn forward two squares because it is the Pawn's first move

African chess set

Now it is Black's turn and he can make his move as though White had moved his Pawn one square only, see *Fig. 39*, and he decides to take White's Pawn. *Fig. 40* shows completion of this move.

Black can only make this capture if he does so immediately after White's escape move. In an actual game, of course, other White Pieces would have been moved before Black's Pawn could have reached the position shown in the diagrams.

This is the En Passant move and it is not nearly so difficult as it sounds. Place the Pieces on your board as shown in *Fig. 37* and when you make the move indicated for Black, remove the White Pawn from the board.

This rule applies to all Pawns and is best thought of as a move to stop Pawns which are making their first move from escaping capture by drawing alongside a hostile Pawn. The escaping Pawn can be taken as if it had moved one square only.

Reproduction Lewis chess set

PLAYING THE GAME

Opening a Game

Once you know the Pieces and the moves which they can make, there is no quicker way of learning chess than by playing a game.

If you do not have an opponent then play against yourself by turning the board round after each move. On the other hand you will probably make faster progress if you can persuade another member of the family, or a friend, to learn with you and act as an opponent.

White always moves first and the decision as to which player has the White Pieces is decided by lottery. It is usual for one of the players to conceal a Pawn of each colour in either hand and then allow his opponent to choose. Whichever colour the player chooses he then plays in his first game. Thereafter the players alternate between White and Black.

Let us now open a game together. Place all your Pieces on the board and make your moves with me. The diagrams will help and you may like to use the numbered board for this exercise. In each case the Piece

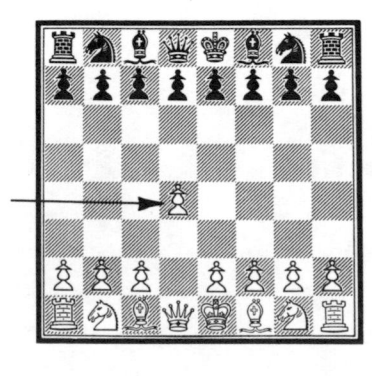 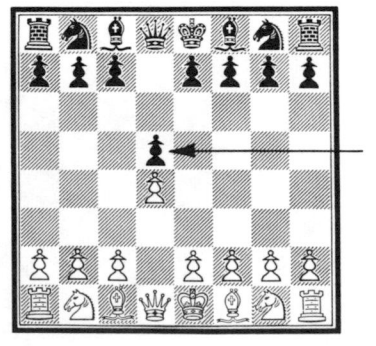

LEFT:
41 White opens with Pawn to Q 4

RIGHT:
42 Black replies with Pawn to Q 4

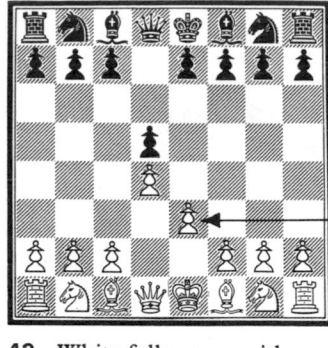

43 White follows up with King's Pawn to K 3. Neither player can take a Piece yet

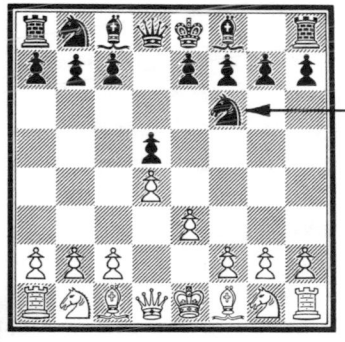

44 Black advances his King's Knight to KB 3 in one move

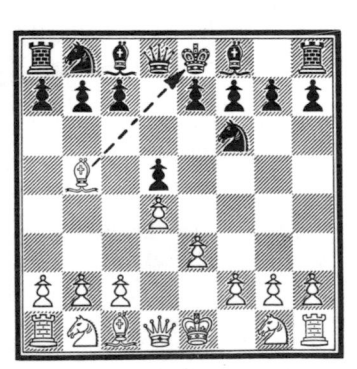

45 White brings out his King's Bishop and this is Check, as the arrow shows

which has just been moved is marked with an arrow from outside the board. A Check or threat to an important Piece is shown with a broken arrow on the board in the diagrams. White moves first and he elects to move his Queen's Pawn to Q 4 *(Fig. 41)*. Black replies with Pawn to Q 4 *(Fig. 42)*, and he has blocked the progress of White's Pawn so that both players are now equal.

It is White's turn to move again and he decides to move his King's Pawn one square to K 3 as *Fig. 43* shows. If he had moved this to K 4, Black could have captured his Pawn.

Because he has moved this second Pawn a square behind his first and can take diagonally, it is protecting the Queen's Pawn. That is to say, White could take any Piece which comes along to capture his Queen's Pawn. What does Black do now? He can, of course, make the same move but if you look at *Fig. 44* you will see that he has brought out his King's Knight. Remember, Knights can hop over other Pieces—your own and your opponent's. This Knight is ready to jump to the square occupied by Black's Queen Pawn should this Piece be taken.

The contestants are about equal. Neither can make a capture in his next move. It is White's turn again and there are a number of things he can do. *Fig. 45* shows that he, too, had decided to get a striking Piece out and has moved his King's Bishop. Because the King's Pawn has been moved out of the way, the diagonal of White squares is clear for him to move his Bishop to QKt 5. He now calls Check because, as you can see in *Fig. 45*, the Bishop is now in direct line of fire to the Black King.

In his next move White would take the King. Black must now get his King out of Check and you will remember that he must:

1   Move his King to a square where he is not under attack.

2   Take the Piece attacking him by occupying the square from which the hostile Piece has been firing at him.

39

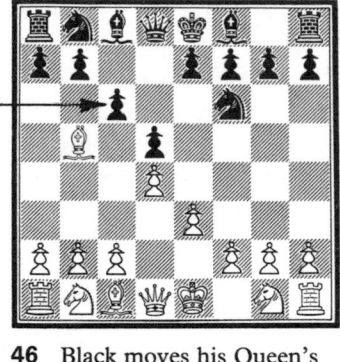

46 Black moves his Queen's Bishop Pawn forward one square placing it between his King and the hostile Bishop. Black is no longer in Check and his Pawn could take the Bishop in Black's next move

3   Call to his aid one of his own Pieces which must remove the attacking Piece.

or

4   Call to his aid one of his own Pieces which must be placed between the attacking Piece and himself.

Look at Black's back row in *Fig. 45*. The King cannot move out of Check because the only square available to him is on the same diagonal as the attacking Bishop and this would not be moving out of Check. Can Black take the Bishop with any of his other men? The answer is no. Certainly the King cannot do the job himself because he can only move one square at a time.

He must therefore place a Piece on the diagonal between the White Bishop and his King.

Fig. 46 shows Black's move. It is Queen's Bishop Pawn one square forward. Black is no longer in Check and he can, in his next move, take White's Bishop unless White first moves the Piece to a safe square. Remember Pawns take diagonally and therefore Black's Bishop Pawn is now in a position to take White's King Bishop. White now withdraws his Bishop to one of four places —the square on which the Piece started, or to either K 2, Q 3 or R 4. In this game, White decides to retreat to Q 3 as shown in *Fig. 47*.

The game proceeds and Black now moves his King Rook Pawn two squares forward as shown in *Fig. 48*. Look carefully at the diagram. White could take this Pawn with his Queen but he does not do so. Why not? What about Black's Knight? Or indeed Black's Rook?

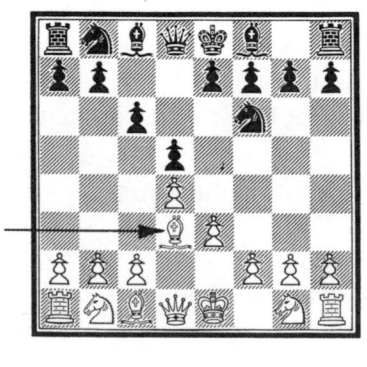

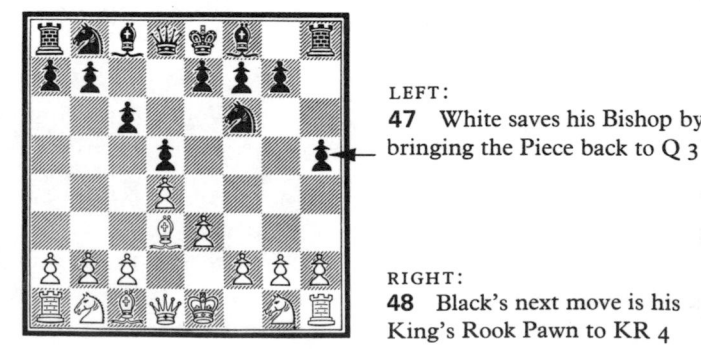

LEFT:
47 White saves his Bishop by bringing the Piece back to Q 3

RIGHT:
48 Black's next move is his King's Rook Pawn to KR 4

49 White replies by blocking Black's Rook Pawn with his own

White does not want to lose his strongest Piece for the sake of a Pawn capture. *Fig. 49* shows that he decided to move his own King's Rook Pawn to KR 4.

Black replies with a challenge to the White Queen. He moves his Queen's Bishop to KKt 5 as shown in *Fig. 50*. If White does nothing to protect his Queen she can be taken in Black's next move. He decides not to take the Bishop with his Queen because she would be lost in the next move to Black's Rook Pawn. Instead White moves his King's Bishop Pawn one square to KB 3 *(Fig. 51)*.

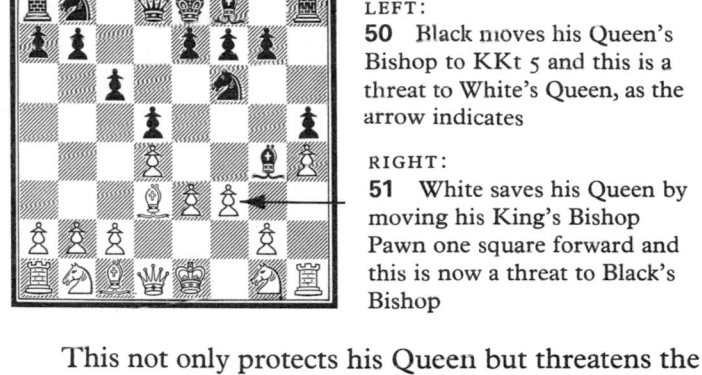

LEFT:

50 Black moves his Queen's Bishop to KKt 5 and this is a threat to White's Queen, as the arrow indicates

RIGHT:

51 White saves his Queen by moving his King's Bishop Pawn one square forward and this is now a threat to Black's Bishop

This not only protects his Queen but threatens the attacking Bishop. Black wisely decides to save his Bishop and moves the Piece to K 3 *(Fig. 52)*.

White now moves his Pawn to QR 4 *(Fig. 53)*. Black brings out his Queen and moves along the diagonal to QR 4 *(Fig. 54)*. This is Check again but it is far from

52 Black saves his Bishop by moving the Piece to K 3

53 White moves his Queen's Rook Pawn two squares forward

54 Black decides to bring out his Queen to QR 4 and calls Check

41

55 White gets his King out of Check by placing his Queen's Bishop between the hostile Queen and his own King

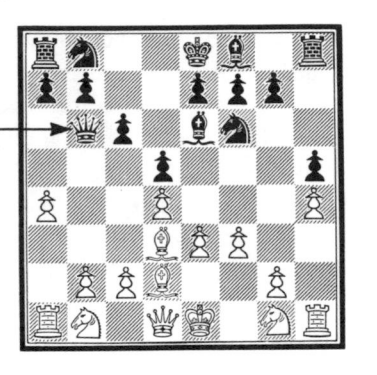

56 Black's Queen was in danger from White's Bishop and you will see that Black has moved her one square on the diagonal path, which puts her out of danger. The game proceeds

Checkmate. What is White's reply? Look at *Fig. 55*. He moves his Queen's Bishop to Q 2 thus interposing a Piece between his King and Black's Checking Piece. This is a threat to Black's Queen and, as you can see in *Fig. 56*, he moves her to QKt 3 and the game proceeds.

Is this a classic game? No, far from it. In fact it was played out to a victory by Black in the thirty-second move by my daughters Pauline and Sarah aged eleven and eight.

Try this opening again. This time see if you can read the game from the following, and try to remember why each move was made in the way that it was.

WHITE	BLACK		WHITE	BLACK
1 P—Q 4	P—Q 4	5	P—KR 4	B—KKt 5
2 P—K 3	KKt—B 3	6	P—KB 3	B—K 3
3 B—QKt 5 ch	P—QB 3	7	P—QR 4	Q—QR 4 ch
4 B—Q 3	P—KR 4	8	QB—Q 2	Q—QKt 3

Checkmate

Let us now look at some chess endings and see how the various Pieces can achieve a Checkmate. To make the diagrams easier to understand all Pieces have been removed from the board except the King, which is under attack, and the attacking Pieces. Look at *Fig. 57*. This is Checkmate from two Rooks.

The White King is under attack from the Black Rook on the back Rank and he cannot escape into the next Rank because of the other Rook. Remember a King must never move into Check so the game is over and Black has won.

Fig. 58 shows a Checkmate by Queen and Rook. White King cannot take Black Queen because if he did

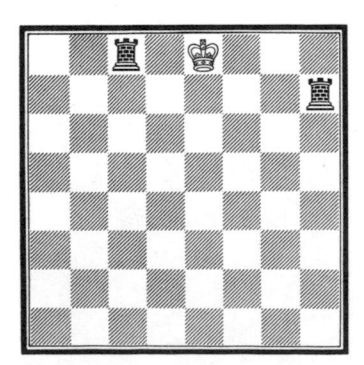

57 White King is Checkmated by the two Black Rooks. He is in Check from the Rook on the back Rank and cannot move into the next Rank because of the other Rook

so he would be moving into Check from the Black Rook. Any of the open squares available to him are also covered by the Queen. Black has won again.

58 White King Checkmated by Black Queen and Rook. He cannot take the Queen because of the Rook in the next Rank and he cannot move to either of the adjoining squares because these are covered by the Queen

59 Black King Checkmated by two Bishops and a White Knight. He cannot move to the White square in the next Rank because of the Bishop, and the adjoining square in the back Rank is covered by the Knight

In *Fig. 59* you can see that Black King is Checkmated by the White Bishops and a White Knight. The King is in Check from the Bishop on the Black diagonal and must move. He cannot go to R 2 because the other Bishop is firing at this square. Alas, he cannot go to Kt 1 because the Knight can take on this square. Black is now Checkmated.

Look at *Fig. 60*. Here the Black Queen has just moved to give Check to the White King. His only escape is to take her but he cannot because this square is covered by the Black Bishop.

Fig. 61 shows a similar situation only this time it is the Knight who is supporting the Queen. Set these Pieces up on your board and try to move the White King out of Check. It cannot be done.

There are, of course, many other combinations which provide a Checkmate and you will soon discover some of these when you start to play.

60 White King cannot move out of Check from Black Queen except by taking her, and this he cannot do because it would mean moving into Check from the Black Bishop. He is Checkmated

61 White King can only get out of Check by taking the Queen, but he cannot move onto her square because it is covered by the Black Knight. He is Checkmated

62 A well-supported Pawn achieves Checkmate. Black King cannot take Pawn because of the Queen. He cannot move to either of the White squares next to him because of the Queen and Bishop

Remember that a Pawn can give Check to a King and can help to Checkmate him. *Fig. 62* shows an example of this.

Black King cannot move in his own back Rank because of the White Queen. He cannot take the Checking Pawn because of the Queen. A well-supported Pawn has produced a Checkmate.

Rules

Finally, here are some rules to observe. Always move a Piece once you have touched it and do not ask your opponent if you may change your mind. If you touch a Piece in order to put it back in the centre of a square always say 'I adjust' or, less formally 'I am only adjusting'. Always take an opponent's Piece once you have touched it—providing it can be taken, of course. There is no penalty if you find you have made a mistake and the Piece cannot be taken.

Drawn Game

Remember that a game can end in a draw. There are two ways that this can come about. One is Stalemate which means that the game cannot proceed. Suppose White was not in Check and it is his turn to move. Imagine also that to move it would put the King in Check. Then the game ends in a draw because this is Stalemate. This applies no matter what the opponent's strength may be at the time.

The second kind of draw is what is known as Perpetual Check. In this case let us suppose White puts his opponent's King in Check. Black moves his King on to a safe square and White Checks him again with the same Piece. Black dodges back to his original refuge. Again White Checks him from the original checking position, and so on. This is Perpetual Check and the game ends in a draw.

Discovered Check

You may find an opportunity to Check your opponent by means of a move known as a Discovered Check. To do this you move a Piece away from a direct path between a striking Piece and your opponent's King. The result is Check but not from the Piece which you have moved.

Look at *Fig. 63*. The Black King is not in Check and it is White's turn. Now look at *Fig. 64*. White has moved his Pawn to a position which does not give Check but Black is now in Check from White's Bishop.

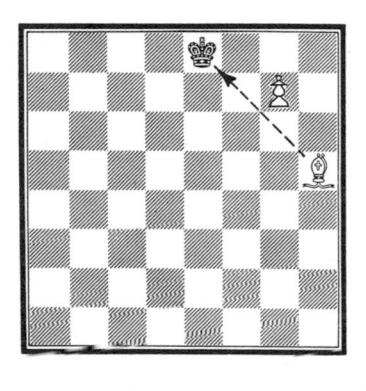

LEFT:

63 Black King is not in Check and it is White's move

RIGHT:

64 White moves Pawn one square forward and Black is now in Check from White's Bishop. This is a Discovered Check. Black King is Checked by a Piece that was not moved to give Check

Another move to watch for is a Double Check. In *Fig. 65* Black is not in Check and it is White's turn. He moves his Rook to give Check and there is a Discovered Check from the Bishop. *Fig. 66* shows the Double Check.

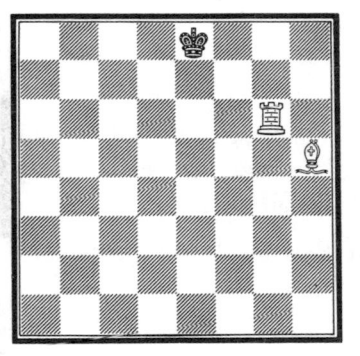

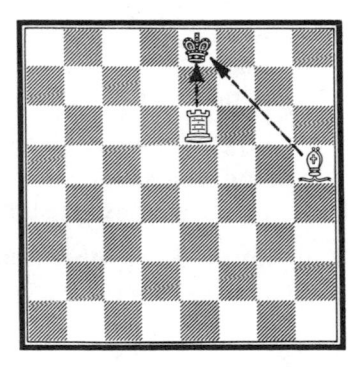

LEFT:

65 Black King is not in Check but if White moves his Rook there will be a Discovered Check from the Bishop

RIGHT:

66 White gives Check to Black King from both Bishop and Rook. This is a Double Check

The more games you play the better player you will become. You would now do well to play a few games before trying to master any more theory. Good play comes from practice as well as study. Perhaps the best way to become a good player is to find a strong opponent and make up your mind to beat him. Plan your attack, anticipate his defence, and keep smiling when you lose!

Some Points to Remember

1 PLAY Only two can play. The players move

alternately and White always starts. Decide by lottery who shall play White.

2 MAKING A MOVE A player should not change his mind once he has made a move.

3 THE BOARD Always make sure you have a White square at the right-hand corner of the board before you start.

4 KINGS One square at a time in any direction is the King's move. He must never move into Check, nor must he move onto a square immediately adjoining that of an opponent's King.

5 QUEENS Remember that Queens always start on squares of their own colour; white Queen on a White square, black Queen on a Black square.

6 BISHOPS One of your Bishops starts and ends on a White square, the other on Black. They always move across the diagonals and can advance or retreat as far as they like if the squares are free.

7 KNIGHTS Only the Knights can jump over Pieces—yours or your opponent's. They go two squares in one direction and one square in another in one move.

8 ROOKS Sometimes called Castles, the Rooks move along Ranks or Files. They can move as many squares as they like and can advance or retreat.

9 PAWNS Remember that Pawns always move one square at a time except on their first move, when they can move two squares. They take diagonally. Pawns never retreat.

10 SACRIFICES Never take a weak Piece with a strong Piece if, in his next move, your opponent can take your strong Piece. Move your Queen carefully and guard her well.

PART TWO

IMPROVING YOUR GAME

THE OPENINGS

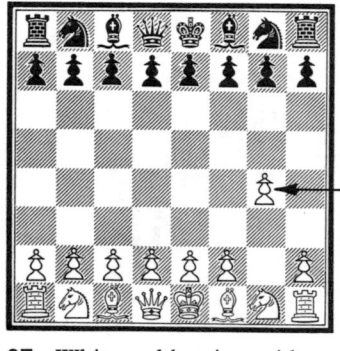

67 White rashly tries a side Pawn opening and paves the way for Black to achieve the Fool's Mate

The Chessboard is a battleground with forces of equal strength arrayed against each other. The players are the generals and the one who uses his forces most cleverly will win.

Some sacrifices are almost inevitable, but the clever general allows these only when he is sure they will contribute to his eventual victory. There are so many variations in the opening moves that it is not possible to tackle more than a very small fraction of them here. Many of these opening moves follow a pattern and to each move there is a known reply. The player must decide from his experience of battles fought which openings suit him best.

A good rule for the beginner is to stick to a centre opening and start with either his King's or Queen's Pawn. If he is playing Black he would be well advised to counter his opponent's move by blocking the progress of the White Pawn's move. This is, of course, a defensive move and leaves the initiative with White, but before long Black will have the opportunity to force the game his way.

The Fool's Mate

There are dangers in unconventional openings and perhaps the most impressive example of this is what is known as the Fool's Mate *(Figs. 67–70)*. Try it out on your board. Here is how it goes:

	WHITE	BLACK	
1	P—KKt 4	P—K 4	
2	P—KB 3?	Q—R 5!	Checkmate

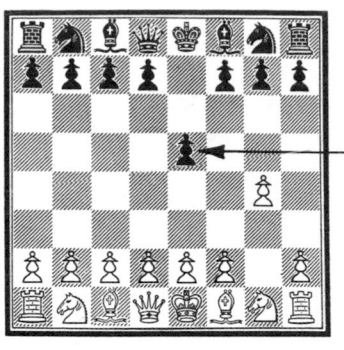

68 Black replies with the conventional Pawn to K 4 opening

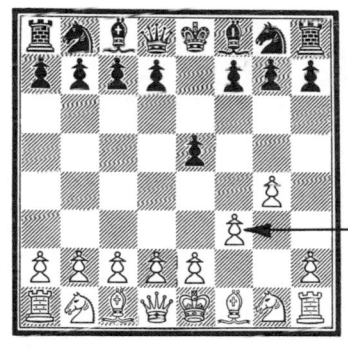

69 White's second Pawn protects his first but . . .

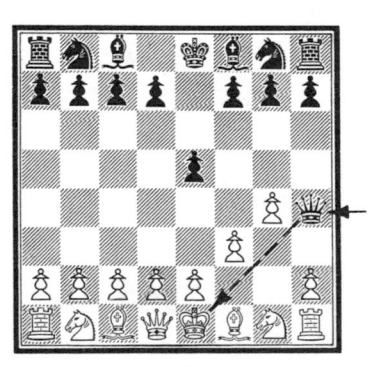

70 Black takes advantage of the diagonal leading to White's King and goes Queen to R 5. Check! Look again—it is Checkmate

In his second move Black has Checkmated White! Foolishly White opened up a diagonal to his King and made a trap for himself. Look at the position. The King cannot move out of Check because if he moves at all it can only be onto the next square of the diagonal along which the Queen is firing at him. This means he is still in Check. Can he intersperse a Piece between the hostile Queen and himself? The answer is no. His Bishop can only move on another diagonal and is powerless to intervene in one move. His Knight can make only one move and that is to KR 3 which leaves the King in Check. His Pawns cannot retreat. White King is Checkmated after only two moves!

This could not have happened if White had kept to a conventional centre opening. However, there is more to opening and developing a game than making two good or bad moves. You will not, normally, defeat your opponent in two moves. Your strategy should be to open up the game by getting out striking Pieces and mounting an attack.

There are advantages to be gained by bringing out Knights in the early moves. It is better to establish a strong position for them in the centre of the board rather than advancing them to the sides. They are slow-moving Pieces but obviously, because of the nature of the Knight's move, it has more mobility and power in central positions. Furthermore, when a Knight has left the back Rank it has helped to clear the space necessary for Castling.

When a King's Knight has left the back Rank, only the Bishop stands in the way of Castling. Bishops are strongest when they operate in unison and if they can be manoeuvred into a side-by-side position they constitute a formidable duo.

Rooks, too, are most useful as striking Pieces when they occupy central positions and this contributes to the desirability of early Castling.

In this one move you are placing your King in a less vulnerable position, as well as bringing one of your second most powerful Pieces towards the centre of the board.

A Standard Opening

Let us now play out a standard opening and see the motive for each move. White elects to open the game on the King's side and starts with P—K 4 *(Fig. 71)*. Black replies with P—K 4 thus blocking the progress of White's Pawn *(Fig. 72)*.

White now brings out his King's Knight and moves Kt—KB 3 *(Fig. 73)*.

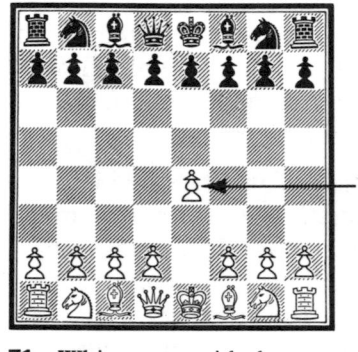
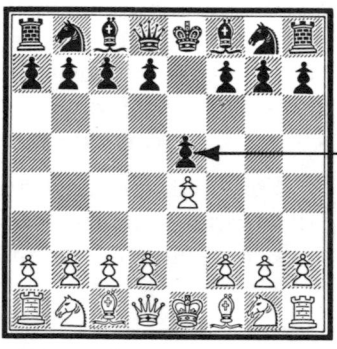
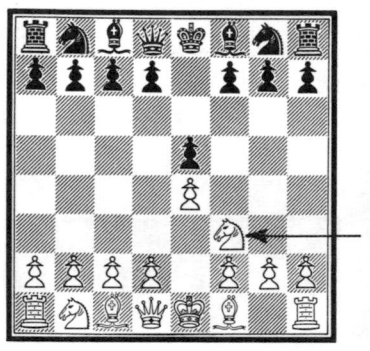

71 White opens with the conventional Pawn to K 4

72 Black replies with the same move thus blocking the progress of White's Pawn

73 White brings out his King Knight which in its next move could take Black's Pawn

Black replies with a similar move Kt—QB 3 *(Fig. 74)*. White now turns his attention to the Queen's side of the board and moves Kt—QB 3 *(Fig. 75)*. Black again follows suit and moves Kt—KB 3. The positions

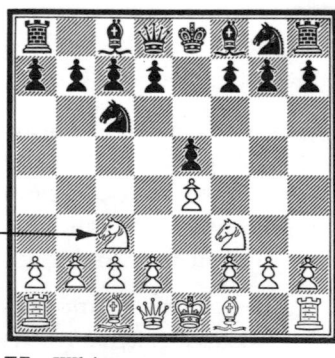

74 Black moves his Queen Knight to the position from which it protects his opening Pawn. If White Knight takes Black Pawn, Black Knight would take White Knight

75 White now protects his opening Pawn by bringing out his Queen Knight

76 Black brings out his King Knight. The position is now equal for both players of the Pieces so far are shown in *Fig. 76.*

Now White moves B—Kt 5 and it becomes clear that he is going to Castle in his next move *(Fig. 77)*. Again Black copies White's move and goes B—Kt 5 *(Fig. 78)*. It is the fifth move and both players Castle.

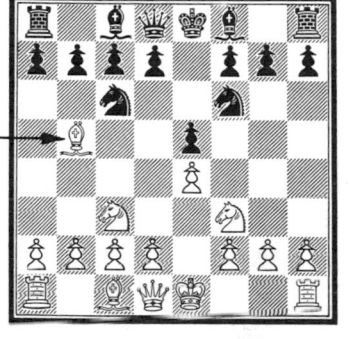

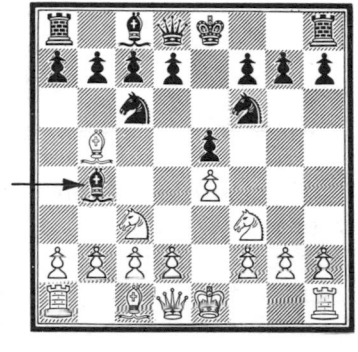

LEFT:

77 White moves his King Bishop to threaten Black's Queen Knight

RIGHT:

78 Black replies with Bishop to Kt 4 and threatens White's Queen Knight. The position is equal again. Note that both players are now free to Castle

Experts advise Castling by the tenth move and in this opening both players have achieved this early. The position is still equal, though White, being the first to move, has the initiative.

Whereas each move so far has been fairly predictable, we cannot be sure of what White will do now. Look at the position as shown in *Fig. 79.* White can now threaten Black's Bishop by P—QR 3, or he can go a stage further in development by P—Q 3 opening a diagonal for his Queen's Bishop. Let us assume that he does the latter. Black can once again follow suit and move P—Q 3 *(Fig. 81)*.

79 Both players Castle

80 White moves his Queen Pawn to Q 3

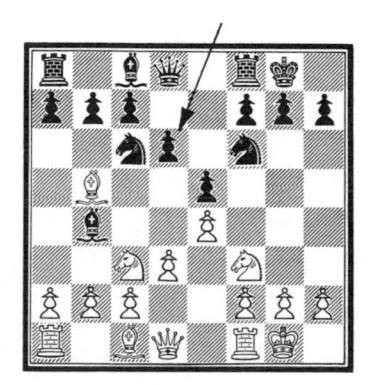

81 Again Black follows suit and goes Pawn to Q 3

51

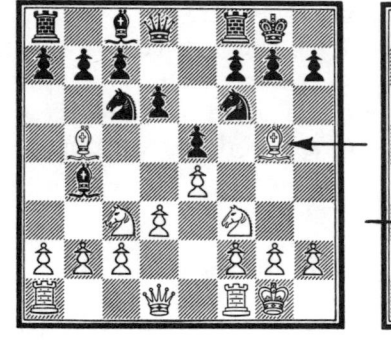 

82 White now brings out his Queen Bishop and threatens Black's King Knight

RIGHT:
83 The slaughter starts— Black Bishop takes White Knight

The position is still equal and White still has the initiative. Having opened the channel for his Queen Bishop, he moves B—Kt 5 *(Fig. 82)*. Black now decides that the time has come to take the initiative from his opponent. Furthermore, he decides to forestall an attack starting with White moving Kt—Q 5 by taking White's Queen Knight with his Bishop. The move is B X Kt *(Fig. 83)*. In doing this he loses his Bishop to a Pawn but, as we know, the value of the Pieces involved is equal so it is a reasonable exchange. The game proceeds and we will not follow it any further. We have learned from this the wisdom of centre moves in opening a game and how to achieve early Castling.

Early Castling

A good general rule is to open the game with a number of your Pieces rather than move one or two Pieces many times. The advantages of this policy are that if you clear the back Rank properly you can Castle early; you bring striking Pieces into play, and you can develop a strong Pawn formation. Beware of early Queen moves. Any Piece brought out into the open part of the board is vulnerable and subject to attack. You cannot afford to lose your Queen and bringing her into play too early may mean your early moves are all devoted to defence instead of development and attack.

We have seen that it is a good general rule to Castle early in the game but remember the conditions which govern your right to Castle. The squares between the King and Rook must be vacant; the King must not be in Check, and you can Castle only if neither King nor Rook has yet made a move in the game.

Original Staunton chess set by Jaques with matching leather chessboard

84 A conventional opening. Both players go Pawn to K 4

Do not be over eager to Castle. You cannot Castle until the fourth move because you must get both Bishop and Knight away from the back Rank. It is necessary to move a Pawn to let the Bishop through, which accounts for the three preparatory moves. During this time your opponent, if he is playing White, has made four moves and these could have been made to mount an attack which you may later find very costly.

Here is an example in which a beginner was too eager to Castle. His opponent had the advantage of a little more experience. The beginner is playing White. He opens with P—K 4 and Black follows suit *(Fig. 84)*.

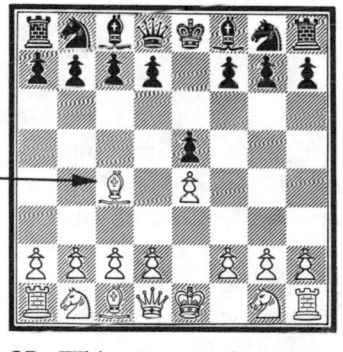

85 White starts to clear his back Rank for Castling by bringing out his King Bishop

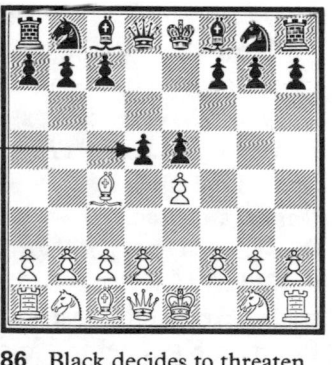

86 Black decides to threaten this Bishop with a Pawn

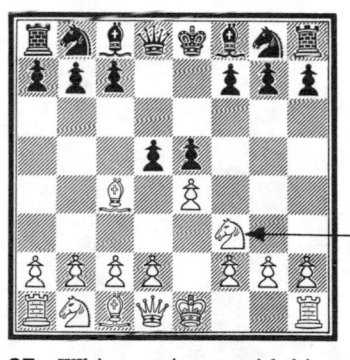

87 White carries on with his plan to Castle by bringing out his King Knight

88 Black Pawn captures White Bishop

White brings out his King Bishop and moves B—B 4 *(Fig. 85)*. Black replies with an early challenge. He moves P—Q 4 *(Fig. 86)* which is a threat to White's Bishop. White is so keen to Castle that he ignores his Bishop's fate and moves Kt—B 3 *(Fig. 87)*, which clears the squares between his King and Rook. Black now takes White's Bishop with his Pawn. The move is P X B *(Fig. 88)*. In this game White is not so experienced as Black and the early loss of a Bishop is only the beginning of his troubles. Let us follow the game a little further because there is as much to be gained from observing the faults of beginners as there is from following the brilliant moves of the masters. The position so far is shown in *Fig. 88*.

Modern chess set and chessboard in glass fibre

89 White persists in his plan and Castles

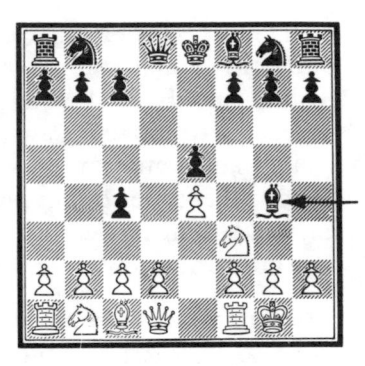

90 Black now threatens White's King Knight

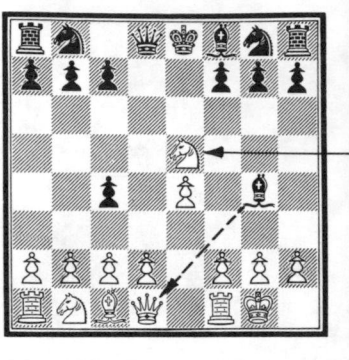

91 White decides to move his threatened Knight to a position from which it could capture Black Bishop but . . .

92 Black Bishop captures White Queen!

Now it is White's turn again and he makes the move for which he has sacrificed so much. He Castles *(Fig. 89)*. Black now starts to mount an attack and moves QB—Kt 5 *(Fig. 90)*. What is the point of this move and what will he do next? White thinks this is an attack on his Knight and unless he moves the Knight he will surely lose it. In fact, Black is too smart to waste a Bishop on taking a Knight at this stage. He would lose the Bishop because there is a Pawn on Kt 2, behind and in the next File. White does not notice this and thinks that he will make the best of things not only by saving his Knight but in the course of doing so by capturing a Black Pawn. White now goes Kt X P *(Fig. 91)*. Black now completes his manoeuvre and moves in to capture the White Queen! *Fig. 92* shows B X Q. Black will now lose his Bishop to White's Rook but no matter, White has lost his Queen and a Bishop. Black's casualties are a Bishop and a Pawn. The player should always remember the relative values of the Pieces and whereas Bishop taking Bishop is a fair exchange, giving one's Queen for a Pawn is a bad bargain.

This question of equal exchanges such as Pawn for Pawn, Bishop for Bishop and so on is very important and should never be far from the player's mind. A poor exchange must weaken the player's strength especially in the opening part of the game. There are situations where quite drastic sacrifices can be made in the end

93 White opens with his Queen Pawn and goes Pawn to Q 4

game if the player sees very real advantage in losing a powerful Piece. Indeed it may clear the way for him to effect a Checkmate. But not in the early part of the game when the player should be thinking of mustering his forces for an attack.

The Queen's Gambit
Let us now look at one more example of opening play. This time I have chosen a fairly common opening which has for many years been popular with master players.

The formula, like many other openings which follow a predictable pattern, has acquired a name. It is called the Queen's Gambit. Here is how it goes. White opens with P—Q 4 (*Fig. 93*) and Black follows suit by blocking White's Pawn. He goes P—Q 4 (*Fig. 94*). White now moves his Queen Bishop Pawn into a position of jeopardy P—QB 4, and the game proceeds as either the Gambit Accepted or Gambit Declined depending on whether Black decides to take White's Pawn or ignore the challenge. Let us assume that Black declines the offer because he knows White can easily get even later on. Black instead plays P—K 3. This is generally considered the wiser move. *Fig. 96* shows the position after Black has moved. He is on the defensive and, though he can equalise if White captures his Queen Pawn, he has blocked the path of his Queen Bishop should White decide to bring out striking Pieces from his back Rank. In this variation we will assume that White does just this and in his third move goes Kt—

94 Black blocks the progress of White's Queen Pawn with his own Pawn

95 Here is the Gambit. White goes Pawn to QB 4. Black is invited to capture White's Bishop Pawn

96 Black declines and moves his own King Pawn to K 3 to protect his opening Pawn

57

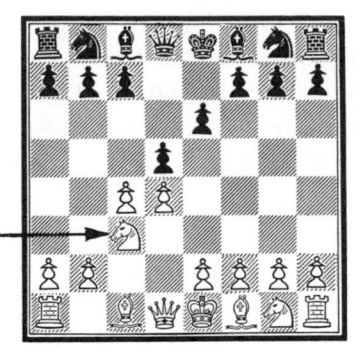

97 White brings out his Queen Knight

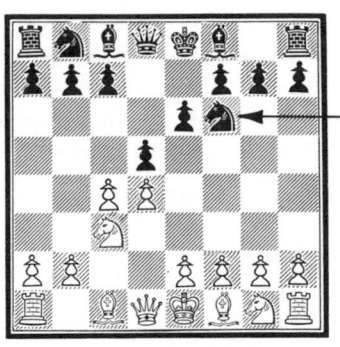

98 Black continues development on the King side and goes Knight to KB 3

99 White Bishop now moves to threaten Black's King Knight

QB 3 *(Fig. 97)*. Black can now either capture White's Pawn or, if he is thinking ahead, he will decide to develop his own back Rank and clear the way for Castling. Black now goes Kt—KB 3. The position is shown in *Fig. 98*. White continues to bring out forces from his back Rank and moves his Queen Bishop to Kt 5 *(Fig. 99)*. Indirectly this is a threatening move, though Black can answer the threat in more than one way. Note that if Black moves his King Knight then his Queen becomes vulnerable. He can, if he wishes, threaten White's Bishop with his Rook Pawn by moving KRP—KR 3. Alternatively he can relieve the pressure by placing his King Bishop on K 2. In this game Black decided to continue development of his back row by bringing out his other Knight and *Fig. 100* shows his move. It is QKt—Q 2. If White decides to capture Black's King Knight the reply from Black would be Kt X B and this is much better than P X B because he does not want to clutter up a File with double Pawns.

It is good practice to play out a standard opening like this and try alternative moves of your own, noting the advantages and disadvantages of these variations. Remember that opening moves are only the beginning of the battle and that most of the exchanges will probably come in the middle and end game.

Before going on to openings on the King's side, let us play out the beginning of the Queen's Gambit Accepted. The less-experienced player is more likely

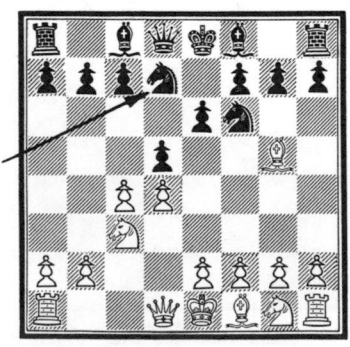

100 Black supports his King Knight by bringing out his Queen Knight

to find this pattern acceptable because chess is a game in which looking ahead plays a very important part and only the experienced player knows when it is possibly best to refuse a proffered Pawn.

Suppose then that Black accepts the challenge and captures White's Queen Bishop Pawn, how will the opening develop now? The moves are White P—Q 4 *(Fig. 93)* and Black follows suit with P—Q 4 *(Fig. 94)*. Again White goes P—QB 4 *(Fig. 95)* and this time Black decides to capture the challenging Pawn. His move is P X P *(Fig. 101)*. Before long White can equalise but first he goes Kt—KB 3 and Black replies with the same move Kt—KB 3. The position so far is shown in *Fig. 102*.

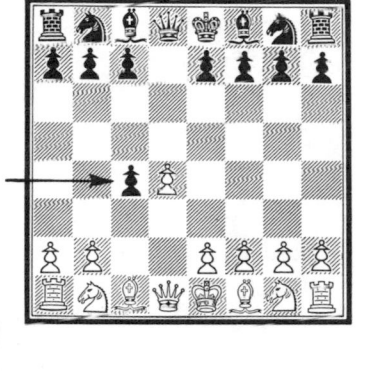

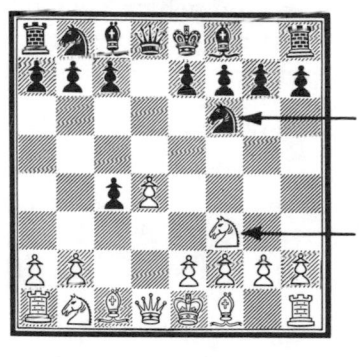

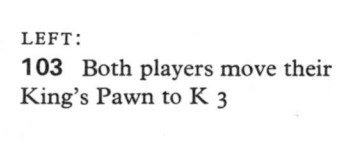

LEFT:
101 Queen's Gambit Accepted—Black captures White's Queen Bishop Pawn

RIGHT:
102 White now goes Knight to KB 3 and Black Knight to KB 3

Both players now bring another Pawn forward and each moves P—K 3 *(Fig. 103)*. White is now in a position to equalise and takes Black's Queen Bishop Pawn and, at the same time, clears the back Rank on the King's side for Castling. White's move is B X P *(Fig. 104)*. The game can now proceed in a number

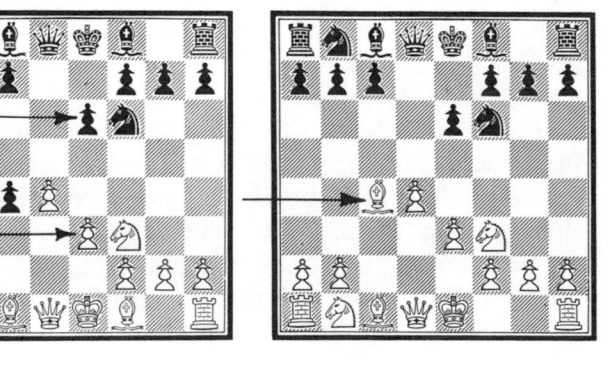

LEFT:
103 Both players move their King's Pawn to K 3

RIGHT:
104 White's King Bishop takes Black's Pawn and equalises

59

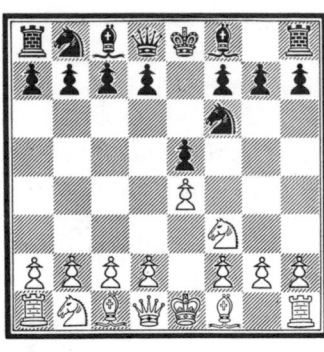

105 The opening moves in Petroff's Defence

106 White challenges Black's King Pawn by moving Pawn to Q 4

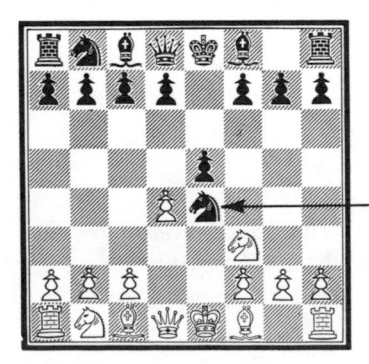

107 Black captures White's King Pawn with his King Knight

of different ways but we have carried it far enough to see that accepting the Queen Pawn in the second move does not necessarily give Black any great advantage. Look at the position now. White has equal strength with Black in terms of Pieces on the board. He is ready to Castle before Black and he has two striking Pieces in central play while Black has only one.

King's Side Openings

As in the case of Queen's side openings there are many openings on the King's side of the board that follow known patterns and have acquired their own names. Perhaps the most popular and widely played is Ruy Lopez. After the first two moves there are a number of variations which have sub-titles such as Bird's Defence, Classical Defence, etc. In many of these White Castles early in the game—usually in the fifth move.

The first moves are:

	WHITE	BLACK	
1	P—K 4	P—K 4	
2	Kt—KB 3	Kt—QB 3	
3	B—Kt 5	Kt—B 3	(Berlin Defence)
		Kt—Q 5	(Bird's Defence)
		B—B 4	(Classical Defence)

Less frequently played, but worth some study, is the opening known as Petroff's Defence. White's first move is P—K 4 and Black follows suit *(Fig. 84)*. White now goes Kt—KB 3 which is a threat to Black's Pawn. Black replies with the same threat to White's Pawn and moves Kt—KB 3. The positions of the Pieces so far are shown in *Fig. 105*. There are now two conventional moves which White can choose from. The first is P—Q 4 as shown in *Fig. 106*, or he can, of course, take Black's Pawn with his Knight. In this example of Petroff's Defence, White elects to challenge the Pawn with his Queen Pawn so Black's next move is Kt X P. *Fig. 107* shows the move completed. An alternative for Black would have been P X P.

White now threatens Black's Knight by going B—Q 3 *(Fig. 108)* and Black's reply is P—Q 4. In this move he comes to the support of his unprotected

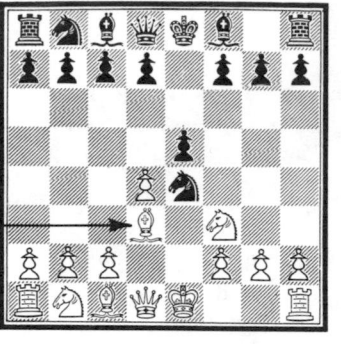

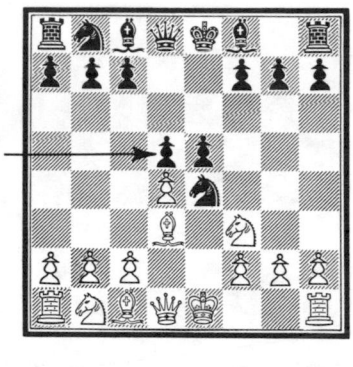

108 White threatens Black's undefended King Knight with his King Bishop and has cleared the back Rank ready for early Castling

109 Black brings up his Queen Pawn to support his King Knight

Knight. If White's Bishop takes Black's Knight, Black's Pawn will capture the Bishop. In fact White takes Black's King Pawn with his Knight *(Fig. 110)*. Look at the positions of the Pieces on the board now. Each player has captured a Pawn. Each has a Knight out in the centre of the board and both Pieces are supported. But White has a Bishop in play and his back Rank is clear for him to Castle. It is Black's move and he goes B—Q 3 *(Fig. 111)*. The players are equal again. Both have Bishops menacing their opponent's Knights. Both are now ready to Castle *(Fig. 112)*.

White now goes P—QB 4 *(Fig. 113)*. Look at the possible moves after this challenge. If Black takes this Pawn with his Queen Pawn, White can equalise with his King Bishop, which is supported by his Knight. But in the next move Black could capture White's Knight with his own King Bishop. In fact Black's reply

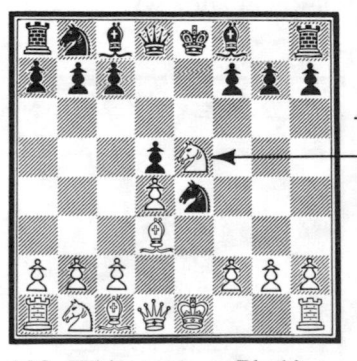

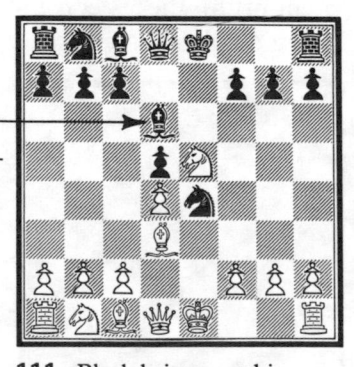

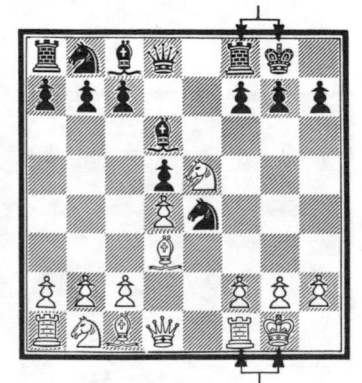

110 White captures Black's King Pawn with his King Knight

111 Black brings out his King Bishop and threatens White's King Knight. Black is now ready to Castle

112 Both players Castle

61

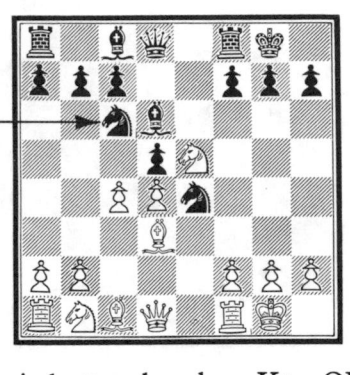

LEFT:
113 White now challenges Black's Queen Pawn. He goes Pawn to QB 4

RIGHT:
114 Black goes Knight to QB 3 ready for more than a Pawn capture!

is better, he plays Kt—QB 3! *(Fig. 114)*.

Now the slaughter starts. White's move is P X P *(Fig. 115)* and Black takes White's Queen Pawn with his Knight as shown in *Fig. 116*. Study this position carefully. If you were playing White what would you do? Note that Black's King Knight is un-supported. The move then is B X Kt *(Fig. 117)*. This is Black's move too! *Fig. 118* shows that Black's Bishop has captured White's King Knight. This is as far as we need take this opening. Study the positions of the Pieces now.

If you aim to become a good player it is well worth memorising some of the standard openings, with special attention to those which seem to suit your own approach to play. Remember that your aim in openings is always twofold—to obtain command of the centre and, at the same time, to give attention to development. From this we proceed to the middle game, in which develop-ment of the Pieces continues and expands with a cam-paign of planned attack.

115 White Pawn captures Black Pawn and now threatens Black Knight

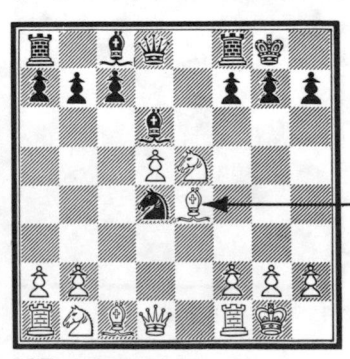

116 Black Knight captures White's Queen Pawn

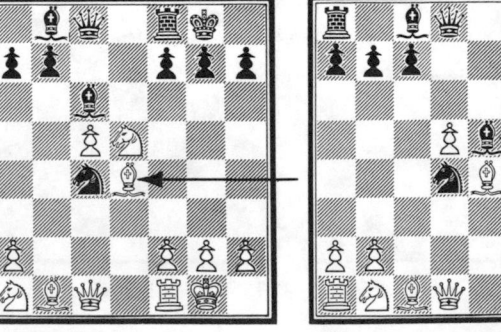

117 White Bishop takes Black Knight and . . .

118 Black Bishop takes White Knight

THE MIDDLE GAME

119 White cannot move his Rook without putting his King in Check. White Rook is Pinned by Black Bishop

Once the opening Pawns have been moved and some of the striking Pieces have taken their positions in the centre of the board the player has the opportunity to develop an attack which, it is hoped, will lead to the trapping and immobilising of the enemy King.

It is dangerous to drift from move to move capturing the occasional proffered Pawn. Your opponent would very quickly manoeuvre you into an untenable position resulting in your King being Checkmated.

Continue development in the middle game but combine the capture of hostile Pieces with a strategy which includes attack upon the enemy King or Queen. If you can capture the Queen without risking your own and, of course, without making too big a sacrifice, you are well on the way to achieving a very commanding position.

Pinning a Piece

Avoid becoming Pinned! This happens when one of your Pieces is forced to remain on its square because it is so placed that it protects another Piece from being captured. Look at *Fig. 119*. All Pieces have been re-moved from the board except those involved in a Pin. Here Black Bishop is threatening White Rook and, assuming Black prefers to move other Pieces on the board, White Rook is Pinned. If it is moved, then White King is exposed to Check and, as you know, the rules forbid a player to expose his own King to Check. The Rook is said to be Pinned.

A Pin can result from attacks other than those on the King. Look at *Fig. 120*. Here again all Pieces have been

120 If White Knight is moved Black Bishop will capture White Queen. White Knight is Pinned

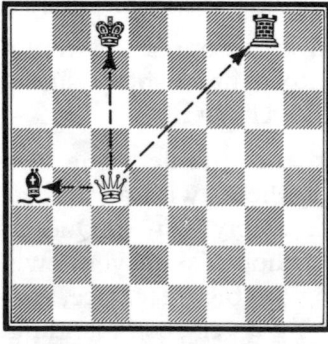

121 Black King is in Check and must move. White Queen can then capture Black Bishop or Rook—very nice Fork

removed except those involved in the Pin we are demonstrating. The White Knight is Pinned. Unlike the previous example, the Piece Pinned may be moved by the player but the result of the move would be a serious loss to White. He would say farewell to his Queen.

When a player finds that he has a Piece on the board that is Pinned he should consider an offensive against the attacking Piece or the possibility of effecting a similar Pin against one of his opponent's Pieces. In either case he must also consider to what extent new strategy will affect his plan. When a player finds that he has had a valuable Piece Pinned on the board it is bound to affect his play, and he would be well advised, therefore, to be on the lookout for opportunities to Pin his opponent.

The Fork

An attack in chess manifests itself in a threat and this can be twofold. Look at *Fig. 121*. Here again, for the sake of clarity, all Pieces have been removed from the board except those needed for the demonstration. It is White's move. The two Black Pieces on the board are both in jeopardy. White can take either Black Bishop or Black Rook. If it were Black's move he would, in any case, have to move his King because it is in Check.

Watch for opportunities to Fork your opponent. Study *Fig. 122*. This is a simple Bishop Fork. It is Black to move and he can capture either Rook. The decision as to which of the two Rooks he could take would be dependent upon the positions of all other Pieces on

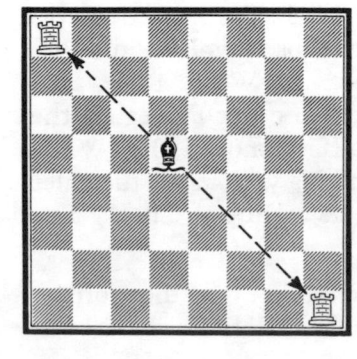

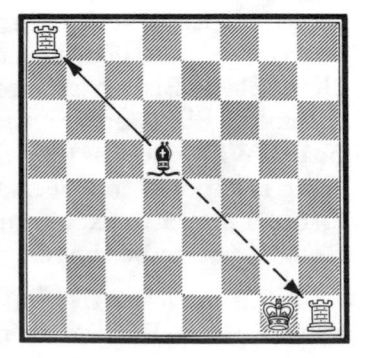

LEFT:
122 Black Bishop can capture either of White's Rooks— useful Fork

RIGHT:
123 Black Bishop captures one Rook and continues to threaten the other

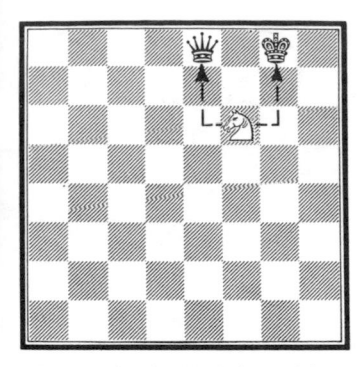

124 A deadly Fork by White Knight! Black King must move. Black Queen is then captured

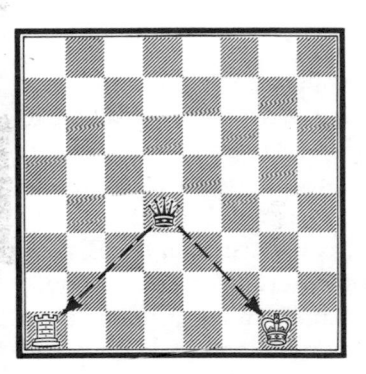

125 White King is in Check and must move. Black Queen then captures White Rook

the board. If you look at *Fig. 123* it becomes clear that Black should go B—QR 1 and not B—KR 8 or he will lose his Piece and the move becomes an exchange instead of a capture.

This consideration must form a part of the player's strategy throughout the game. In the middle game when each player is working from an opening towards the end game, he will have opportunities to capture or exchange. With certain exceptions a capture usually strengthens his position whereas an exchange leaves both players a little weaker. However, your opponent may offer you a Piece by placing it in jeopardy—a gambit whereby he may gain more than he loses through capturing something of greater value than the Piece he 'gave' you.

There are many different Forks; be wary of these. *Fig. 124* shows a Knight Fork. Here White Knight calls Check and when Black moves his King, White's move is Kt X Q. White may then lose his Knight to Black's King but in terms of strength he has gained from the move.

A Queen Fork is shown in *Fig. 125*. White King is in Check and must move. Black Queen is now able to mop up Black's Rook. If other Pieces were still on the board the result might be very different of course and this is why the player must study the relative positions of all Pieces involved in any attack or defence.

Much can be gained from reading and studying chess books but this should go hand-in-hand with practice. Theory is one thing, knowledge gained from practical experience is another, and the middle game offers more opportunity for learning from actual experience in play than either the openings or the end game. There are so many combinations that the most exhaustive book could only scratch the surface, and trying to memorise so much theory would only prove irksome.

It is helpful to the beginner to play regularly against a stronger opponent. It may be disappointing to lose nearly every game but this must not be allowed to dishearten the player. Practice may not make perfect but it will certainly improve one's play.

THE END GAME

A good opening and skilful play in the middle game should lead to victory in the end game and this we will now examine. The object is to Checkmate your opponent, which you know from the earlier examples is a matter of trapping the hostile King. It is not sufficient to trap the King if you merely manoeuvre him into a position from which he cannot move, unless in so doing you are able to call 'Check'. In other words, if a player finds that he cannot move without putting his own King in Check, this is a Stalemate.

Stalemate

The simplest example of a Stalemate is shown in *Fig. 126*. The White King is not in Check and it is White to move. Where can the King go? He cannot move left or right in his own Rank because to do so would be to move into Check from Black's Bishop. He cannot capture Black's Bishop because, as you can see, the Bishop is guarded by Black's Queen and here again White would be moving into Check. He cannot move into the next Rank because of the Rook Pawn which blocks him and the Queen which is guarding the Bishop.

Clearly White King is immobilised but he is not, repeat *not*, in Check. This, then, is a Stalemate and the game is a draw. Look at the respective forces involved in this end game. White has, apart from his King, only one Pawn on the board. Black, too, has a Pawn but this is supported by both a Bishop and his Queen. Despite Black's superior forces he has allowed a situation to develop which has made his victory impossible. White has been very lucky to draw even with his opponent at the end.

126 This is typical Stalemate. White King is not in Check and it is White to move. Neither White King nor White Pawn can move. Result —a draw

66

Checkmate

It is worth studying the requirements for a Checkmate in terms of Pieces needed. Towards the end of play it could be that only very few Pieces are left on the board and, at this stage, you must decide whether or not you or your opponent can Checkmate.

If the slaughter in the middle and end game has been severe you may well find that, whereas your opponent has only his King left, you are reduced to a Bishop and King. You cannot effect a Mate with these Pieces and the game is a draw. The same applies if you are reduced to a King and Knight or indeed a King and two Knights against a lone King. To achieve Checkmate against a lone King you must have not less than one of the following combinations: King and Queen; King and Rook; King and two Bishops or King, Knight and Bishop. These are minimum requirements and obviously the job will be easier and quicker if your striking material is stronger. It should be mentioned that a King and three Knights can produce Checkmate although this is an unlikely combination. Remember that a Pawn which reaches the eighth Rank can be changed for any of the more powerful Pieces and there is no reason why you should not elect to promote such a Pawn to a Knight. Most players elect to 'Queen' such Pawns.

We have studied some simpler Checkmates, let us now see what can be done if fewer Pieces survive than in the combinations already discussed.

Firstly a King and Queen against a lone King. Look at *Fig. 127*. Black King and Queen must Check White King which is not in Check at the moment. *Fig. 128* shows how it is done. Black Queen has moved to the same Rank as White King putting him in Check. White King cannot escape because he must move into the next Rank and he cannot do so because the only three squares available to him are those adjoining the squares on which Black King stands. As you know, the rules insist that there must always be one square between Kings. To effect this Mate the King and Queen must work together to drive the hostile King to a Rank or File at the edge of the board.

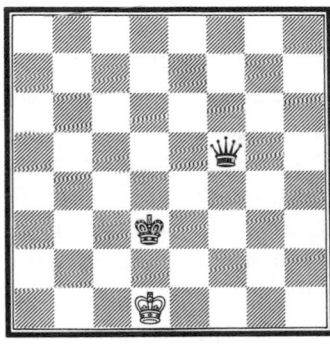

127 King and Queen against King. White King is not in Check but it is Black's turn to move

128 Black Queen puts White King in Check and he cannot move because Black King guards the three squares in the Pawn Rank. Checkmate!

67

129 White King cannot move out of Check because his only escape is to capture Black Queen. Black King protects her. Checkmate!

130 King and Rook against King. Black King keeps White King in the back row and in Check. Checkmate!

Previous examples of Checkmate have shown that if a Queen is placed on an adjoining square to the hostile King at the edge of the board the only escape for the King is to capture the Queen. If he cannot do this he is Checkmated. *Fig. 129* shows how King and Queen working together can achieve this sort of Checkmate. White King cannot take Black Queen because of the rule forbidding Kings to occupy adjoining squares. If he moves left or right in his own Rank he is still in Check from the Queen.

Now let us see how a King and Rook can achieve Checkmate on their own. Look at *Fig. 130*. Here the Black Rook has just put the White King in Check. What escape is there for White? He must leave the back Rank but the only squares available to him are those three which would mean his occupying a square adjacent to the hostile King.

And now let us see what Bishops can do. We know that one Bishop and King cannot produce Checkmate but if you have both Bishops on the board you can Mate. Here is how it goes. Your two Bishops, aided by your King, must drive the hostile King to the edge of the board and your King should take up a position one square away from the hostile King. Your Bishop now closes in for the kill. *Fig. 131* shows Black King cornered but not in Check. It is White to move and he goes KB—Q 5 Check! *(Fig. 132)*. Note that your King plays a vital part in these Checkmates. Two Bishops cannot do the job unaided.

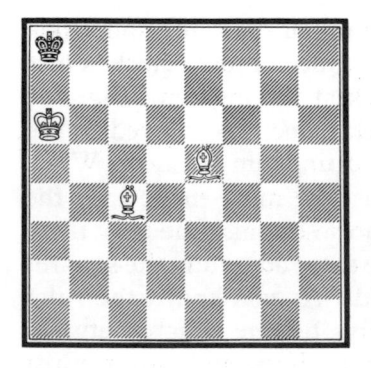

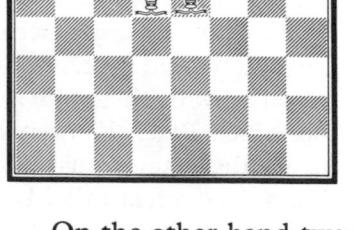

LEFT:
131 King and two Bishops against King. Black is not in Check and it is White to move

RIGHT:
132 Checkmate. Black King cannot leave the back row because of the position of White's King

On the other hand two Rooks against a lone King can very soon trap him. Look at *Fig. 57*. This shows a

Checkmate with two Rooks. The hostile King must be driven to the back Rank and the Rooks then move in for the kill. Look at *Fig. 133*. Here the Black King is away from his own back Rank and White Rooks must drive him back. It is White to move so he goes R—Q 7 Check *(Fig. 133)*. Black cannot move forward in his File because of White's other Rook. He cannot remain in the Pawn Rank so he must move back. He goes K—KB 1 *(Fig. 134)* and all that now remains is for White to go R—R 8 Check. It is all over. Black King has been Rooked! *(Fig. 135)*.

133 Two Rooks against King. Black King must now go to the back row because he is in Check

134 Black King is now trapped in the back row

135 Black King is in Check again and, because of the other Rook, cannot leave the back row. Black King is Rooked!

If you do not have both Rooks left on the board you can Mate with only one. You will, however, need the assistance of your King. In this manoeuvre it is again necessary to drive the hostile King to the edge of the board. Your King can help to do this because, whereas a King cannot Check another King, he can be placed so that the moves of the hostile King are limited because there must always be one square between Kings.

Fig. 136 shows White King driven to the edge of the board with Black King opposite him and only one square between them. It is Black's turn and he uses his Rook to Checkmate White by going R—R 7 Check! *(Fig. 136)*. White King cannot leave the edge of the board because if he does he moves to a square directly adjoining that of the enemy King which is forbidden. It is useless to move in the File because this will not remove the Check from Black's Rook.

136 Black King and Rook Checkmate White King

Finally what about Checkmate from King, Knight and Bishop? *Fig. 137* shows Black King where he was left after Castling. White King has come across the board and is now on KR 6. Black King is not in Check but it is White's move. He goes B—K 6 Check! *(Fig. 138)*. Where can Black King go now? White Knight prevents him from a move left or right in his own Rank and White King stops him from leaving the back Rank. It is Checkmate.

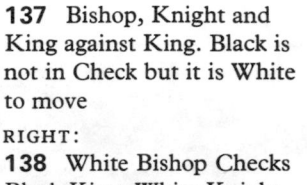

LEFT:

137 Bishop, Knight and King against King. Black is not in Check but it is White to move

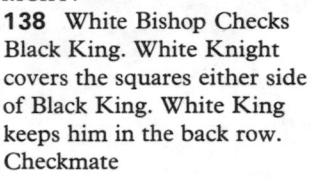

RIGHT:

138 White Bishop Checks Black King. White Knight covers the squares either side of Black King. White King keeps him in the back row. Checkmate

Experienced players seldom let a game go as far as this. When it becomes obvious that you cannot win and your opponent has the necessary strength to Checkmate your King you may, if you wish, resign.

Beginners would do well to press on to the very end because they cannot be sure that, having failed to retain enough strength to win the game, they may yet be lucky and force a draw. In order to test your opponent's ability to Checkmate it is just as well to carry on to the bitter end in your early games. You will very soon learn whether or not you are really beaten.

It sometimes happens that at the end of a game you find that your opponent calls Check after every move you make. This is known as Perpetual Check and the result is then declared a draw.

A Complete Game

Now for a complete game from a Ruy Lopez opening to Checkmate in the twenty-ninth move. White opens with P—K 4 which is shown in *Fig. 71,* and Black's reply is the same *(Fig. 72)*. White now goes Kt—KB 3

Chinese chess set and lacquer chessboard

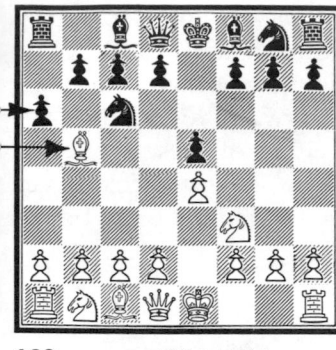

139 MOVE 3 White Bishop threatens Black Knight. Black Rook Pawn comes up to threaten White Bishop

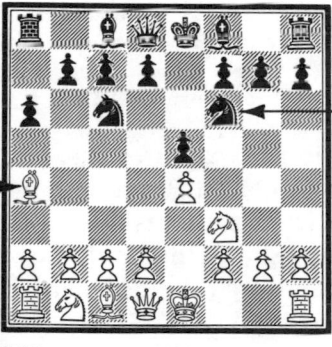

140 MOVE 4 White saves his Bishop and Black brings out his King Knight

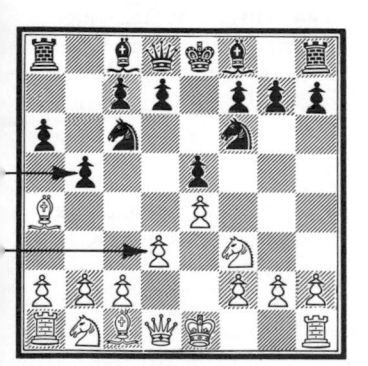

141 MOVE 5 White protects his King Pawn by Pawn to Q 3. Black harasses White Bishop by Pawn to QKt 4

and *Fig. 73* shows the move. Black's reply is Kt—QB 3 and if you look at *Fig. 74* you will see that Black's Knight is guarding his opening Pawn. Suppose that Black had followed suit and moved his King Knight to KB 3. In this position each Knight is threatening to take the opponent's opening Pawn. However, Black prefers to guard his Pawn so that if White were foolish enough to capture it, Black would be rewarded with capturing White's King Knight!

From now on follow the game from *Fig. 139* and note that each diagram shows the moves of both White and Black. As always White moves first and his third move is B—Kt 5. He is doing two things in this move; not only is he threatening Black's Knight but also clearing his back Rank so that he can Castle. The pace of the game, as you will see, is such that White fails to Castle until much later and, because of this, gets into trouble.

Black's third move is P—QR 3 *(Fig. 139)*. White should have expected this and he must now save his Bishop. To withdraw on the same diagonal would serve no useful purpose. To change course, and at the same time keep to the diagonal which leads to Black's King, could, however, prove a profitable move.

White's fourth move is B—R 4 *(Fig. 140)*. If Black intends to hound White's Bishop he has only to move his Queen Knight Pawn to QKt 4 and if White accepts the challenge he loses his Bishop to Black's Rook Pawn in the following move. In fact Black is more concerned with early development of the game so brings out his King Knight.

White is all ready to Castle but Black has yet to move his King Bishop. On the other hand, Black now has a Knight threatening White's King Pawn which is not, as yet, protected. It is the fifth move and White's turn. He goes P—Q 3 *(Fig. 141)* and thus comes to the support of his King Pawn. It is a defensive move which has delayed his Castling. Black now goes P—QKt 4. This is the challenge to White's harassed Bishop.

Again White's chance to Castle is postponed and he saves his Bishop by B—Kt 3 *(Fig. 142)*. Black replies

Rare French chess set with original leather chessboard

with B—B 4 thus clearing his back Rank preparatory to Castling. It is now the seventh move and White goes P—B 3 *(Fig. 143)*. This move anticipates Black bringing his Queen Knight forward to either Kt 5 or Q 5. If Black now makes either of these moves he loses his Knight to White's Pawn. In fact Black moves P—Q 4 and this is a challenge to White's King Pawn.

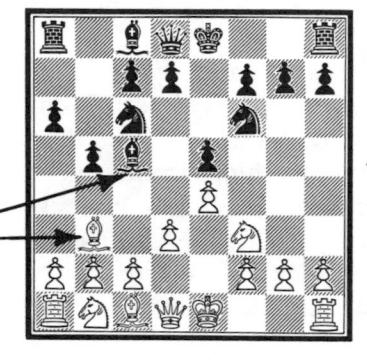

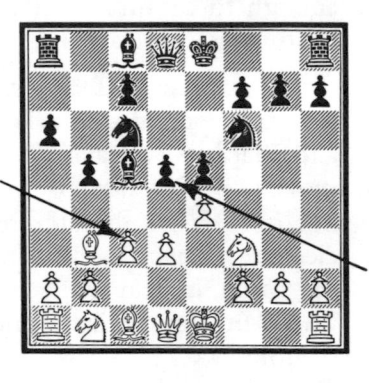

LEFT:
142 MOVE 6 White Bishop retreats. Black King Bishop advances to QB 4

RIGHT:
143 MOVE 7 White moves Pawn to QB 3. Black challenges White's King Pawn by going Pawn to Q 4

The eighth move sees the first capture. *Fig. 144* shows that White takes Black's Queen Pawn with his King Pawn and Black immediately captures this Pawn with his King Knight. *Fig. 145* shows the ninth move and for White it is Q—K 2 and again he has delayed Castling. Black replies by Castling.

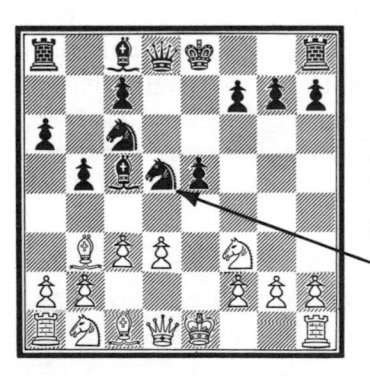

LEFT:
144 MOVE 8 White King Pawn captured Black Queen Pawn so Black has replied by taking White King Pawn with his King Knight

RIGHT:
145 MOVE 9 White decides to move his Queen to K 2. Black Castles

White now goes Q—K 4 and Black B—K 3. White threatens Black's Knight and Black now protects this Knight with his Bishop. In the eleventh move White Knight takes Black's King Pawn and Black immediately captures White's Knight with his own Queen Knight *(Fig. 147)*. White Queen now takes Black's

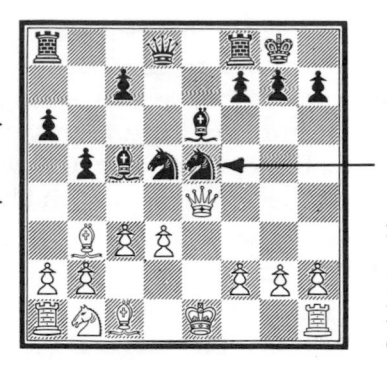

LEFT:
146 MOVE 10 White
Queen moves to the centre of
the board. Black Bishop
moves to K 3

RIGHT:
147 MOVE 11 White
Knight has taken Black's King
Pawn and Black Knight
captures White Knight

Knight and Black goes Kt—Kt 5. Look at *Fig. 148.*
Black's Knight is now in jeopardy because of White's
Queen Bishop Pawn but if White does take this Knight,
Black could reply with B X P Check. In fact White, at
long last, Castles. *Fig. 149* shows the move and Black's
reply Kt X QP.

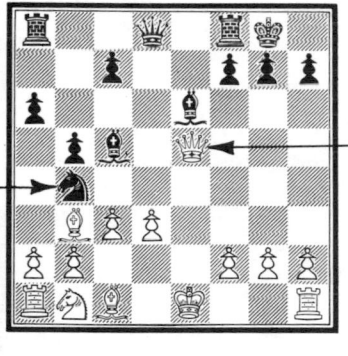

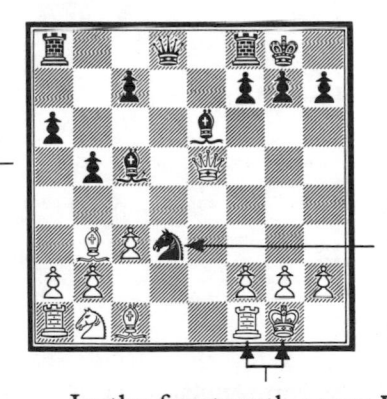

LEFT:
148 MOVE 12 White
Queen takes Black's Queen
Knight and Black's King
Knight moves to QKt 5

RIGHT:
149 MOVE 13 White
Castles at last. Black Knight
advances to Q 6 and captures
White's Queen Pawn

In the fourteenth move White takes his Queen to
R 5 and Black Bishop takes White Bishop *(Fig. 150).*
White's Rook Pawn immediately evens things up

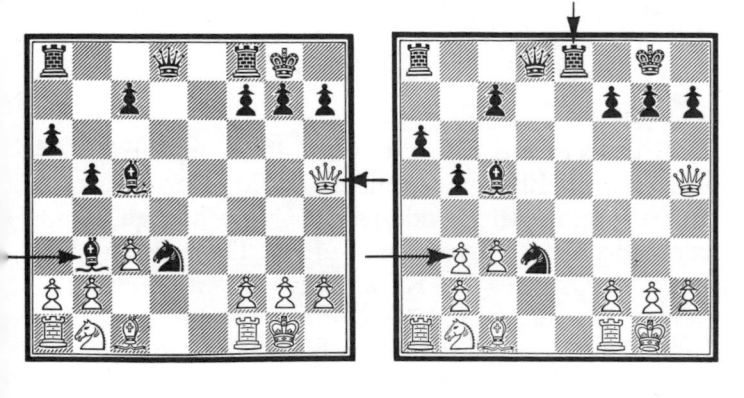

LEFT:
150 MOVE 14 White
Queen goes to KR 5. Black
Bishop captures White Bishop

RIGHT:
151 MOVE 15 White Pawn
captures Black Bishop. Black
moves his King Rook to K 1
in preparation for an attack

152 MOVE 16 White moves his Queen Knight to Q 2. Black continues the development of his attack with Queen to K 2

by taking this Bishop and Black goes R—K 1 *(Fig. 151)*. Now White goes Kt—Q 2 and Black Q—K 2 *(Fig. 152)*. Look at the positions of the Pieces left on the board. The captures have been equal. Both have taken a Bishop, a Knight, and two Pawns. But Black now has his troops more favourably positioned.

Fig. 153 shows the seventeenth move. For White it is P—QKt 4, which is a threat to Black's Bishop, and Black's reply is to hit back with a Pawn capture and a Check. The move is B X P Check. Note that Black's Bishop is guarded by his Knight. Already things are getting difficult for White. His King cannot capture and he will lose his Rook to Black's Knight if he goes R X B.

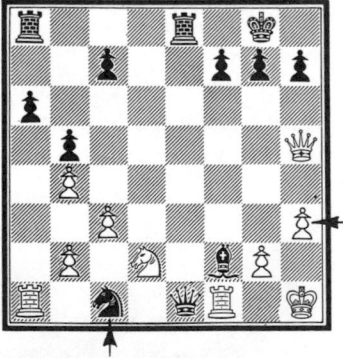

155 MOVE 19 White does not capture Black Queen. He opens an escape route for his King with Pawn to KR 2. Black ignores his Queen's plight and goes Knight to QB 8!

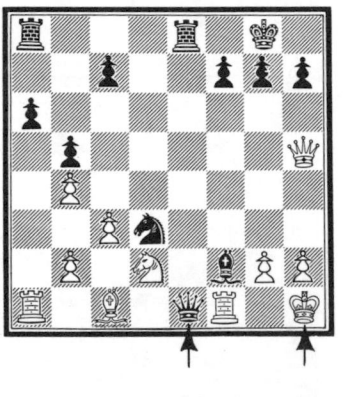

LEFT:
153 MOVE 17 White moves Pawn to QKt 4. Black Bishop captures White Pawn and calls Check
RIGHT:
154 MOVE 18 White King moves to QR 1—the only square available to him. Black Queen sweeps across the board to suicidal danger but this sacrifice will win the game for Black

White now decides to move out of Check to the only square available. He goes K—R 1 and Black's surprise move is Q—K 8! This is a sacrifice but it will lead to Black's victory.

It is the nineteenth move and White ignores the Queen's challenge but opens an escape route for his King. He goes P—R 3 and Black replies with Kt X B *(Fig. 155)*.

In this twentieth move White Rook captures Black Queen and Black Rook takes White Rook—Check. *Fig. 156* shows the position so far. Now White's escape route becomes a temporary refuge. He goes K—R 2 but Black moves B—Kt 8 Check again *(Fig. 157)*. White can only go K—Kt 3 *(Fig. 158)* but as soon as he has done so Black Checks him again. His move is

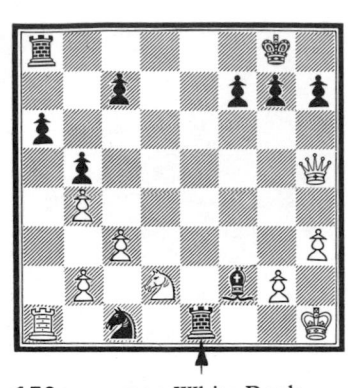

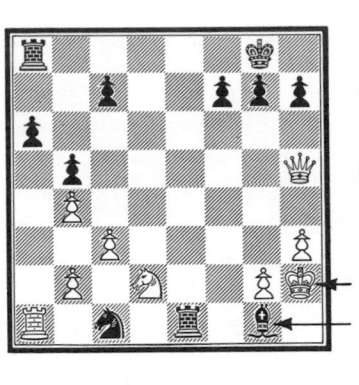

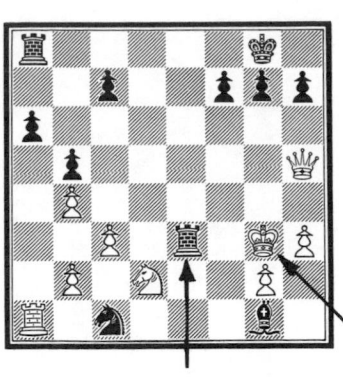

156 MOVE 20 White Rook now captures Black Queen and Black Rook takes White Rook—Check!

157 MOVE 21 White King retreats to QR 2 and Black Bishop advances to KKt 8—Check again!

158 MOVE 22 White King now goes to KKt 3 and Black Rook to K 6—Check!

R—K 6 Check. Look at the board now. Black is without his Queen but his position is stronger than White's. Black is attacking and White is defending.

It is now the twenty-third move and White retreats towards his Queen by K—Kt 4 and Black goes Kt—K 7 as shown in *Fig. 159*. This leaves Black's Bishop exposed to attack from White's Rook but if White goes R X B, Black replies with Kt X R. Alternatively Black could Check White first with R—Kt 6. In the event White decides Kt—B 1 is his move and Black goes P—KKt 3 *(Fig. 160)*. This threatens White's Queen.

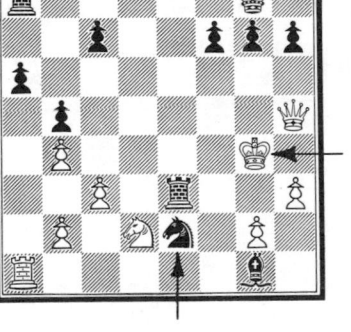

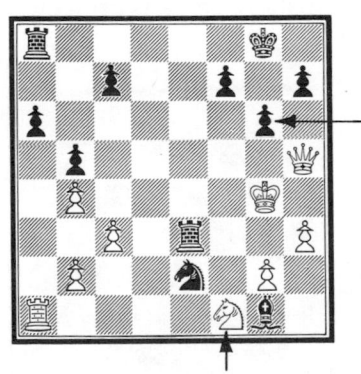

LEFT:
159 MOVE 23 White King is on the run again and goes to KKt 4. Black Knight moves to K 7

RIGHT:
160 MOVE 24 White Knight moves to menace Black Rook by going Knight to KB 1. Black threatens White Queen with Pawn to QKt 3!

White now goes Q—Q 5 and Black P—R 4 Check *(Fig. 161)*. White must move his King again. Move twenty-six is K—Kt 5 for White and K—Kt 2 for Black *(Fig. 162)*. White's King is retreating while Black's starts to advance. Now White Knight takes

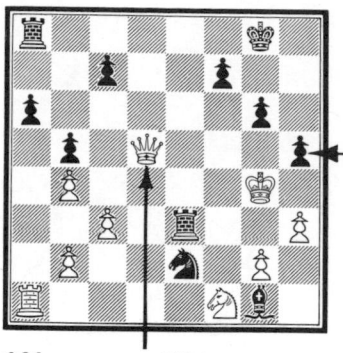

161 MOVE 25 White Queen is now on the run and goes Queen to Q 5. Black Rook Pawn moves to KR 4. Check!

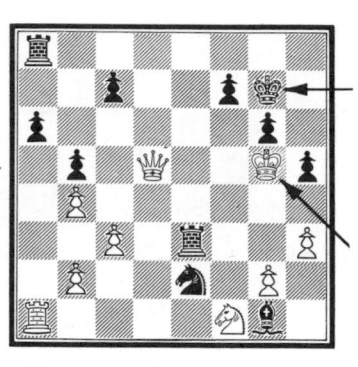

162 MOVE 26 White King is still on the run and goes to KKt 5. Black King advances to KKt 2

163 MOVE 27 The end draws near. White Knight captures Black Rook but Black Checks White King with a Pawn!

Black Rook but Black replies with another Check. He goes P—B 3 Check *(Fig. 163)*. The end is near. It is the twenty-eighth move and White goes K—R 4 and Black B—B 7 Check *(Fig. 164)*.

The last move is shown in *Figs. 165 and 166*. White stops the Check by bringing up a Pawn to stand between the attacking Bishop and his King. The move is P—Kt 3, but look at Black's reply! *Fig. 166* shows Black's triumphant final move. It is B X P Checkmate! The White King is trapped because he cannot take the Bishop which is protected by Black's Knight, he cannot

164 MOVE 28 White King retreats to KR 4. Black Bishop moves to KB 7 and calls Check!

165 MOVE 29 White places his Knight Pawn between attacking Black Bishop and his King. A forlorn move

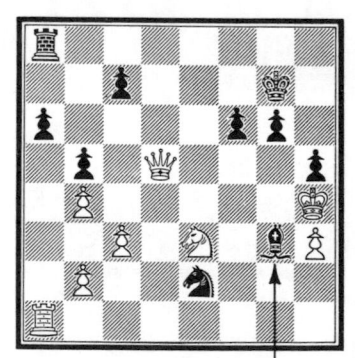

166 MOVE 30 Black Bishop calls Check and cannot be captured. White King is Checkmated!

move in the Rook File because of the Pawns, and to go to either of the squares in the Knight File would be moving into Check.

This was a brilliant ending by Black and it is not too hard to find the point in the game where he achieved mastery over his opponent. In the eighteenth move he placed his own Queen in jeopardy and lost her to White's Rook in the twentieth. Nevertheless this sacrifice was worthwhile. White was able to use his Queen in only one move after this and, in the end, he might just as well have not had a Queen on the board. With great skill and persistent attack Black drove White to ultimate defeat.

For the record, the reader may like to know that this game was played in a New York Tournament in 1889 by two master players, Max Weiss who played White and W. H. K. Pollock who played Black.

There are a number of lessons to be learned from studying a game by master players. In this one we can trace White's ultimate difficulties to a point in the middle game when Black felt strong enough to sacrifice his Queen. Note that experienced players like these do not inevitably capture every Piece that is offered. *Fig. 154* shows the eighteenth move when Black made the apparent sacrifice of his Queen but White's reply was a Pawn move to save his trapped King. Black did not attempt to rescue his Queen but preferred to capture White's Bishop. Only then, in the twentieth move, did White take Black's Queen.

Keep playing chess and one day you may be making moves like these, and winning every—well, nearly every—game.

ABOUT THE PIECES

Staunton Chess Pieces

Chess pieces internationally known as the Staunton type were designed by Nathaniel Cook, a friend of the celebrated English master player Howard Staunton, in 1835. Mr. Cook used symbols in their plainest form; a crown, a coronet, a mitre, a horse's head, a tower, and for the pawns, a simple ball. Each symbol was mounted upon an elegant tapering stem rising from a wide, heavy, circular base to give stability. John Jaques, the chief of a well-known and long-established firm engaged in the manufacture of games and sports equipment, was so highly impressed with the design that he immediately took out a copyright and the type was manufactured on a commercial scale.

Every original Staunton chess set bearing the engraving 'JAQUES, LONDON' is of the very highest quality throughout. Wooden sets were made from heavily weighted boxwood and ebony, and exceptionally fine sets were turned from the finest quality African ivory. Today, in every country of the world where serious chess is played, the Staunton type is regarded as the absolute standard. This can be seen on the jacket photograph and the illustration on page 53.

Chinese Chess Pieces

For upwards of one hundred and fifty years, highly decorative chess sets have been carved from Indian ivory in and around Canton. Chinese craftsmen manufactured these sets in vast numbers; all were destined for the Western markets. Several different types were made, but all follow the same general design. Individual sets differ in size and quality and, as a general rule, the overall quality, of both material and workmanship, improves with size. The pieces of one side were dyed red, green or black, and in rare cases such as the set illustrated on page 71, every piece of both sides has been carefully polychromed.

Modern Chinese Chess Set

In post-war years, large numbers of chessmen have been produced in China where the manufacture is again proving to be a sound commercial undertaking. Only the best sets are worthy of consideration among collectors, although vast numbers of small, poor quality sets are carved from the hollow end of tusks. Modern Chinese sets are usually dyed brown or straw colour, but the set illustrated on page 17 is of exceptional quality and is dyed green.

Modern Chinese Ball Mounted Chess Set

Carved in ivory, the Cantonese concentric ball has been known for centuries. It originated in Canton and, although to the uninitiated the actual carving appears most complex if not impossible, in actual fact skilled craftsmen make little of the task. For at least one hundred and fifty years Chinese craftsmen have used concentric balls as supporting stands for chess figures. One side of each set is stained deep or light brown. Apart from ornamental value, small and otherwise unimportant figures attain some significance and charm when ball-mounted, and where labour is cheap and material costly the extra work is relatively unimportant. Almost all modern ball-mounted sets are manufactured in Hong Kong. See page 18.

French Chess Set

From the beginning of the 18th century French craftsmen have made excellent chess sets from a variety of substances. Ivory, bone, and many types of wood were used to exceptional advantage in the production of many fine sets still in existence. The set illustrated on page 72 is carved from kiln-dried bone with the pieces of both sides finished in colour. This was made in Dieppe not later than the middle of the 18th century and is shown complete with its original leather chessboard.

African Chess Set

Carved from thornwood and ebony, this is a modern chess set made in Tanzania where many small, decorative objects are now carved in vast quantities. Modern African chessmen are expertly carved from good quality materials. See page 35.

Modern Chess Set and Chessboard

From remote times, various different substances have been used in the manufacture of chessmen. Craftsmen of many countries continue the search for new materials to this day, with the emphasis on stainless steel and plastics. The chess set illustrated on page 54 is a fine, clean-cut modern set complete with chessboard made of glass fibre, and is included in the book to illustrate the potentials of modern materials when skilfully used.

Reproduction Lewis Chess Set

Perhaps the most celebrated chess pieces known are those called the Lewis pieces of which seventy-eight pieces exist. These came from at least seven different sets which were all found in an underground chamber on the west coast of the Isle of Lewis in 1831. Sixty-seven are in the British Museum, the remainder in the Museum of Antiquities, Edinburgh. They have been given an Icelandic origin and have also been attributed to craftsmen working in Scotland. Many experts regard these chess pieces as 11th or 12th century, others give them a much later date but, whatever their age, they are altogether distinctive, as can easily be seen from the illustration on page 36.

GLOSSARY OF CHESS TERMS
INDEX

GLOSSARY OF CHESS TERMS

Castle A special move in which the player may move both King and Rook in the one move. Rooks are sometimes called Castles.

Check When the King is attacked by a hostile Piece he is said to be in Check. It is customary for the player to say 'Check' to his opponent when he places a Piece on a square from which it is attacking the King.

Checkmate When a King is attacked and he cannot ward off or escape from the attack, he is Checkmated and the game is over.

Development Bringing out Pieces to positions on the Board where they will be more effective in attack or defence than if left on the squares from which they start.

Discovered Check If a Piece which is not Checking the enemy King is moved, thereby putting the King in Check from another Piece, the move is known as a 'Discovered Check'.

Double Check When the King is in Check from two Pieces at the same time.

End Game The final moves which end in a Checkmate, a resignation or a draw.

En Passant A move allowed to prevent a Pawn escaping capture in its first move by going forward two places and drawing alongside an enemy Pawn. The hostile Pawn can capture it on the square it would have occupied if it had moved forward only one square.

Exchange Moves in which each player in turn makes a capture.

File The pathway of squares leading from the player to his opponent. There are eight Files.

Forced Move When no other move is open to a player he makes a 'forced move'.

Fork When an attacking Piece can elect to capture either one of two pieces in its next move. For example a Queen can capture a Rook by moving on the diagonal or a Bishop in the File.

Gambit A move of a Piece (usually a Pawn) in the opening game when the player offers the Piece in the hope of gaining later from an early loss.

Middle Game The moves in the game when the Pieces have taken their positions and the player has the opportunity to develop an attack and, possibly, trap the enemy King.

Open File A clear File which is not blocked by any Pawns.

Opening The early moves in the game. These usually follow a fairly predictable pattern and most have acquired names, e.g. Ruy Lopez, Queen's Gambit, etc.

Pin To pin a Piece means to force your opponent to keep a Piece on the square it occupies because if he moves it he exposes another, possibly more valuable, Piece to attack.

Rank The rows of squares running from left to right across the Board. There are eight Ranks.

Stalemate When a King is not in Check but is forced to move into Check and therefore cannot move.

Threat A move in which the player so places a Piece that in his next move he can make a capture.

INDEX